POLICY AND PRAC͟ ͟ ͟ ͟ ͟ ͟UCATION

EDITORS

GORDON KIRK *AND* ROBERT GLAISTER

EARLY CHILDHOOD EDUCATION
The New Agenda

J Eric Wilkinson
Professor of Education, University of Glasgow

DUNEDIN ACADEMIC PRESS
EDINBURGH

Published by
Dunedin Academic Press Ltd
Hudson House
8 Albany Street
Edinburgh EH1 3QB
Scotland

ISBN 1 903765 17 X
ISSN 1479-6910

British Library Cataloguing in Publication Data
A catalogue record for this book is available from the British Library

Typeset by Patty Rennie Production, Portsoy
Printed in Great Britain by Cromwell Press

IC. ND PI. TICE IN. ..IION

NUMBER SIX

EARLY CHILDHOOD EDUCATION

The New Agenda

POLICY AND PRACTICE IN EDUCATION

To Sandra, Neil, Adrian and Lynn

CONTENTS

EDITORIAL INTRODUCTION

Education is now widely regarded as having a key contribution to make to national prosperity and to the well-being of the community. Arguably, of all forms of investment in the public good, it deserves the highest priority. Given the importance of education, it is natural that it should be the focus of widespread public interest and that the effectiveness and responsiveness of the educational service should be of vital concern to politicians, teachers and other professionals, parents and members of the general public. If anything, the establishment of Scotland's parliament, which has already affirmed education as a key priority, will witness an intensification of public interest in the nature and direction of educational policy and the changing practices in the schools. This series of books on *Policy and Practice in Education* seeks to support the public and professional discussion of education in Scotland.

In recent years there have been significant changes in every aspect of education in Scotland. The series seeks to counter the tendency for such changes to be under-documented and to take place without sufficient critical scrutiny. While it will focus on changes of policy and practice in Scotland, it will seek to relate developments to the wider international debate on education.

Each volume in the series will focus on a particular aspect of education, reflecting upon the past, analysing the present, and contemplating the future. The contributing authors are all well established and bring to their writing an intimate knowledge of their field, as well as the capacity to offer a readable and authoritative analysis of policies and practices.

The author of the sixth volume in the series is Professor J Eric Wilkinson of the Faculty of Education in the University of Glasgow

Professor Gordon Kirk
Vice-Principal
The University of Edinburgh

Dr Robert T D Glaister
Faculty of Education
and Language Studies
The Open University

ACKNOWLEDGEMENTS

The contents of this book — its ideas, its concerns and its contentions — have emerged from a complex interplay over many years between knowledge, experience and reflection. The knowledge I owe to others. The experience I owe the time others have afforded me, whilst reflection has been a process of necessary and willing indulgence. I am indebted to those who, in a professional context, have contributed to my journey, in particular Johanna Brady, Kay Carmichael, Peter Moss, Helen Penn and Joyce Watt.

On a more personal note but in many ways just as influential, I wish to thank the following who, in their own very idiosyncratic ways, have contributed to my thoughts: Richard Shakir Bulos, Jan De Brun, Kirk Houston, Graham Ramsay, Keith Watson and Peter Wilson.

However, with unreserved appreciation I wish to thank my secretary — Anne Currie. She has re-worked many drafts without complaint.

The search for a more humane society in which awareness, understanding and tolerance are universally appreciated is a daunting pursuit. It is increasingly being recognised that the seeds of such humanity are sown in early childhood. How we engage with young children therefore is of vital importance as it has such a profound impact on both our present and our future. To all those who are involved with young children and who contribute to this pursuit, I owe my respect.

J Eric Wilkinson
January 2003

Chapter 1

INTRODUCTION:
FROM THE OLD TO THE NEW AGENDA

1.1 Setting the Scene

In her book *Early Education: The Current Debate Watt* (1990) set out a number of critical issues in the provision of services for the education of young children in Scotland. These were: co-ordination and continuity of services; the curriculum; and teacher professionalism. She also raised issues concerned with the social context of education, that is, parents and communities. On the issue of co-ordination, concern was expressed not only in Scotland but throughout the UK about the division between 'care' and 'education' in early childhood services. Not only were care and education given different priorities in different kinds of early years settings — day nurseries, nursery schools and classes, playgroups, and family centres — they underpinned the duality of professional qualifications in the field, that is, nursery nurses and nursery teachers with the former being identified as having primary responsibility for the care of children and the latter with their education. But the co-ordination issue was more complex. Given the fragmentation and uneven spatial distribution of early childhood services in Scotland, there was a tension between the three different types of provider — the public sector, the independent sector and the voluntary sector. Many parents were confused about the most appropriate provision, where available, for their child.

If the calls for co-ordination were more directed at the politicians — both local and national — the pressures for curriculum reform delved deep into the professional province of nursery teachers. As shall be seen later in this chapter, the Conservative governments' zeal for control of the curriculum in the period 1979–1997 proved ground-breaking. The drive for national curricular guidelines in the formal school sector in Scotland in the late 1980's was paramount. It was only a matter of time, therefore, before the traditions of early childhood education would be challenged.

But if national curriculum guidelines for early childhood education were just round the corner in the early 1990's there was also concern for what it meant to be a professional in early years services. What were the bodies of knowledge and practice appropriate to being a professional educator in the early years? How would such professionals relate to parents and others on the issue of power and control? These were critical questions raised by Watt in 1990. They are still relevant today.

The publication of Watt's book was followed two years later by Penn's (1992) critical examination of Strathclyde Region's controversial policy on the co-ordination and integration of early childhood services. Penn not only argued for a comprehensive, coherent and flexible service for families with children under 5 years of age but for a radical transformation of the ideology underpinning such services. Only very recently have the initiatives described in *Under Fives: The View from Strathclyde* (Penn, 1992) been taken seriously by central government in Scotland in the report *For Scotland's Children* (Scottish Executive, 2001).

Four years after the publication of Watt's first book on early childhood education in Scotland, she edited a second book specifically focused on 'quality' issues in early education. Following successive Conservative governments' drive for greater accountability in public services in the 1980's and early 1990's by pursuing the improvement of quality, it was appropriate that quality matters should be brought to the attention of early childhood professionals in Scotland. In many respects Watt's second book was the herald for a major concerted effort to improve services in Scotland through a mechanism of quality assurance. All three major players in the provision of education and care for young children invested considerable energy and resources into developing and implementing quality assurance schemes in the late 1990's.

Despite the concerted efforts of many during this period (see, for example, Cohen 1988), to lobby the Government to invest significant funds to expand pre-school provision, the UK was a relatively low provider of state-funded services for young children and their families (see Table 1.1). The UK, along with Portugal, was ranked as the worst provider of services in Europe. Many children living in Scotland did not have the opportunity to benefit from early childhood education before they started formal school, although the voluntary sector at that time did a sterling job to provide sessional places in playgroups and mother/toddler groups. Unfortunately, as services were so sparse and fragmented, children were often subjected to several types of settings each day — especially if the child's parents had full-time employment. As shall be seen later, all this was to change following the election of a Labour Government in Britain in 1997. This event marked a very significant watershed in the development of the early childhood sector of education throughout the UK.

Table 1.1: Places in publicly funded childcare services in selected European Countries in the 1980's as % of all children in the age group

	Date to which Data refer	For children under 3	For children from 3 to compulsory school age	Age when compulsory schooling begins
Germany	1987	3	65–70	6–7 years
France	1988	20	95+	6 years
Italy	1986	5	85+	6 years
Netherlands	1989	2	50–55	5 years
Belgium	1988	20	95+	6 years
Luxembourg	1989	2	55–60	5 years
United Kingdom	1988	2	35–40	5 years
Ireland	1988	2	55	6 years
Denmark	1989	48	85	7 years
Greece	1988	4	65–70	5½ years
Portugal	1988	6	35	6 years
Spain	1988	?	65–70	6 years

Source: Moss, P (1990) Childcare in the European Communities 1985–1990, EC.

1.2 The 1990's Agenda

Returning to the critical issues raised by Watt (1990), Penn (1992) and others, such as Cohen and Fraser (1991) and Pugh (1998 and 2001), it is important from a policy perspective to review the main developments in early childhood education in Scotland during the 1990's. The main developments were concerned with **curriculum**, **co-ordination**, **accessibility** and **quality**.

Towards Curriculum Guidelines

Prior to 1985, matters concerning the school curriculum — planned, organised and sequenced activities for all learners — were, to a large extent, left to the various professional organisations, universities, colleges and the examination board, though civil servants and Her Majesty's Inspectors in the Scottish Education Department at that time made bold attempts to re-orientate the schooling of children in the primary and early years sectors, examples being *Primary Education in Scotland* (SED, 1965) — The Primary Memorandum — and *Before Five* (SED, 1971). By and large, however, central governments were content to leave professional matters to the 'experts'.

With the election of a Conservative Government in 1979, however, a sea-change was set in motion with regard to the relationship between government and the professional and administrative classes. The New Right agenda to raise standards in education in the 1980s required direct involvement in professional matters by central government. Armed with the propaganda of falling standards, central government could no longer stand aside. It had to set a new direction. In 1985 the third report of the Education, Science and the Arts Committee of the House of Commons, *Achievement in Primary Schools*, legitimised the way for the UK Government to determine the education agenda.

The response of the Government to this report led to the introduction of the National Curriculum in England and Wales and the Curriculum Guidelines 5–14 in Scotland. It is significant to note that the Government used legislative procedures in England — the 1988 Education Act — to enforce its will on schools as far as what should be taught and how it should be assessed whereas, in Scotland, a more relaxed approach was adopted. As an alternative to legislation the Government decided to leave it to the Scottish Office Education Department to develop curriculum guidelines. No one is in any doubt, however, that the 'guidelines' approach has had a major impact on what is taught in primary schools in Scotland in terms of breadth and balance in the curriculum, without the necessity of legal enforcement.

Following the consultation paper on *Curriculum and Assessment in Scotland: a Policy for the 90's* (1987) a series of Review and Development Groups, consisting mainly of professional educators, proceeded to generate curriculum guidelines for children aged 5–14 in Scotland. In general, these guidelines were welcomed by teachers and others, though there was fierce resistance to the additional proposal for the national testing of children at ages 7 and 11.

To a large extent the national curriculum guidelines for children aged 5–14 did not impact directly on the pre-school years although, at the time, there was a great fear that a centralist approach to schooling would be 'downloaded' into the early years sector. Early childhood education professionals saw themselves as guardians of a child-centred curriculum. As Watt put it: *The child-centred curriculum is at the heart of early education* (Watt, 1990, p 78). Nevertheless, the introduction and implementation of national curriculum guidelines presented a serious challenge to the child-centred curriculum which involved:

> Putting the child's own development, needs and interests at the centre of the curriculum; learning by discovery, experience and problem-solving; and play as the medium of education. (Watt, 1990, p 78)

In 1990 Watt claimed that the curriculum in early childhood education *may be reaching an important milestone in its development*. This 'milestone' was not long in coming.

Some two years later Her Majesty's Inspectors of Schools in the Scottish Office Education Department (SOED) published a report *Education of Children Under 5 in Scotland* (SOED, 1994). The report paved the way for the introduction of national curriculum guidelines in the pre-school year. A fundamental feature of the report was the claim that in a range of different settings, early education staff were agreed about the over-arching aims for pre-school education (See Fig. 1.1).

Figure 1.1: Aims of pre-school education in Scotland

- provide a safe and stimulating environment in which children could feel happy and secure
- encourage the emotional, social, physical, creative and intellectual development of children
- promote the welfare of children
- encourage positive attitudes to self and others and develop confidence and self esteem
- create opportunities for play
- encourage children to explore, appreciate and respect their environment
- provide opportunities to stimulate interest and imagination
- extend children's abilities to communicate ideas and feelings in a variety of ways

Source: Education of children under 5 in Scotland, SOED, 1994.

This 'agreement' was seen as the *raison d'etré* for moving the nursery sector towards national curriculum guidelines in the year before formal school started.

In 1996 the draft version of the guidelines, in the form of a Curriculum Framework, was launched for consultation. Surprisingly, the draft guidelines were welcomed by practitioners and others, perhaps because they enshrined the principles of a child-centred curriculum, taking as their starting point the needs of the child. The following year saw the publication of the final version of the guidelines which, on the face of it, enshrined the child-centred approach:

> The curriculum refers to a framework of planned learning experiences based on different aspects of children's development and learning. (SOEID, 1997a)

Aspects of children's development and learning identified in the Curriculum Framework were:

- emotional, personal and social development
- communication and language
- knowledge and understanding of the world
- experience and aesthetic development
- physical development and movement

All nursery establishments in Scotland across the different types of provider — the local authorities, the voluntary sector and the independent sector — were encouraged to implement the guidelines. As with the 5–14 curriculum guidelines, *A Curriculum Framework for Children in their Pre-school Year* was widely accepted and subsequently served to drive the regulatory requirements of HMI inspections of state-funded nurseries (see Chapter 6).

Co-ordination
Provision of education for families with children under 5 years of age in the UK prior to 1997 was widely acknowledged to be woefully inadequate in three main respects: availability, organisation and inequity. Reference has already been made to the low level of provision in Britain prior to 1997. Not only were many 3- and 4-year olds unable to gain access to nursery provision but the situation for under-threes was dire. Only about 2% of under-threes had access to services, mainly in the independent sector.

Even where provision was available, however, there were immense shortcomings and inequalities in the existing system of early childhood education and care. As Moss and Penn put it:

> The present hodgepodge of provision fails to deliver flexible, multi-functional and equally accessible services. (Moss and Penn, 1996, p 46)

This hodgepodge was largely the legacy of successive post-war governments' failure to provide the necessary resources to expand the system, despite an apparent willingness to recognise the need for such services. (See, for example, *Education in Scotland: A Statement of Policy*, SED, 1972). Unfortunately, it was all too easy for governments to cite the argument that children's needs should be the prime responsibility of the family and not the state. Given the serious under-funding, local authorities were faced with stark choices of where to locate provision. Some local authorities declined to accept any responsibility for early childhood education whilst others engaged in an ambitious expansion programme of new nurseries, even though provision in such nurseries was almost entirely part-time, i.e. a child would have a morning or an afternoon place, 3 hours per day, five days per week during school terms.

Within the system itself, there were also serious difficulties. Inequity was rife. Some services were regarded as primarily 'educational', for example, nursery schools and nursery classes in primary schools. Such provision was the responsibility of the Education Department in local authorities. Other services were to provide welfare for children living in families with social problems. These day-nurseries and family centres were provided and administered by the Social Work Departments in local authorities. Furthermore, in the staffing of early childhood provision in Britain, there were two professional groups — nursery nurses and nursery teachers. Nursery schools were required to have a fully qualified nursery teacher as head, whilst there was no requirement for a nursery teacher to work in a day nursery. The pay and conditions in the two professional groups were immensely different, and remain so at the present time. Nursery nurses are paid at a significantly lower rate than nursery teachers and often have to work longer and more days per year.

Concerted efforts were made at national level to try and persuade the post-1979 Conservative governments of the need for a national co-ordinated policy on early education and care. Cohen, in her study of services and policies for childcare and equal opportunities in the UK, gave a clear lead and called for the establishment of a national policy and programme:

> A coherent and comprehensive national policy is required for child-care provision for all children. A primary objective should be that of meeting the needs of both parents and children through good quality free or low-cost services in which care for working parents and the stimulation of learning and development are in general seen as common rather than specialised functions. (Cohen, 1988, p 113)

Similarly Moss, in his capacity as Co-ordinator of the European Childcare Network, made out a strong case for robust government action:

> ....there is an urgent need now to review early childhood services in the UK. Such a review should lead to the formulation of a policy to develop an integrated, coherent and comprehensive early childhood service for children from 0 to 5 or 6 years over the next 10–15 years and a programme to implement that policy. (Moss, 1995, p 3)

In her book on developing a co-ordinated approach to early childhood services, Pugh argued:

> The issue of co-ordination has not been neglected in the last decade but progress has seemed depressingly slow. Many commentators have pointed to a lack of government policy, inadequate funding, an absence of leadership. (Pugh, 1988, p 15)

Despite the powerful voices calling for government action, it was left to the local authority sector to take forward the co-ordination agenda, with specific focus on the integration of services. The most recognised of such initiatives was taken in Strathclyde Region with the publication of the Member/Officer Group report *Under Fives* in 1985. The report recommended that the management of early childhood services should be re-organised, and all services, whether previously provided or regulated by social work, should be administered and managed from within the Education Department. It also recommended that a new type of nursery be developed — a community nursery. As Moss put it:

This concept of a *community nursery* was a deliberate attempt to simplify the conflicting values and cut through the professional interests involved in delivering services to pre-fives. (Moss, 1995, p 8)

These nurseries were described by Penn as

The flagships of the Council's philosophy on pre-fives. (Penn, 1992, p 46)

It was intended that the new nurseries would offer high quality pre-school provision that would:

- be open 8 a.m. to 6 p.m., Monday — Friday for 52 weeks per year
- take children from birth to five years on a flexible basis to suit the needs of families based on the Region's admissions policy
- employ all staff (teachers and nursery nurses) on the same conditions of service
- employ local experienced childcarers not necessarily professionally qualified
- be managed by a head not necessarily a teacher
- work with all the relevant agencies concerned with children, including the voluntary sector.

Inevitably, such radical proposals (the first such proposals to appear in Scotland) generated a heated debate. Criticism and resistance abounded, not least from the teaching establishment, particularly the Educational Institute of Scotland (EIS), which regarded these new nurseries as demoting teaching and diluting traditional nursery education. As Penn stated:

What is at issue is the hegemony of nursery education and its supremacy and discreteness as a service to young children. (Penn, 1988, p 119)

She went on to state that the new nurseries:

are seen to be doubly threatening because they demand that formal teaching skills be re-evaluated and further suggest that nursery schooling itself may no longer be the most appropriate service to meet tomorrow's needs. (Penn, 1988, p 120)

Sullivan, the then assistant secretary of the EIS, is reported in the Press 1989 as saying that, as a trade union, the Institute could not accept conditions which would entail teachers working longer hours for less pay and with shorter holidays. In addition, concern was also expressed that the quality of provision in nurseries not run by a qualified teacher would plummet to the level of a 'baby-sitting' service, an issue still causing concern in 2002 (see Chapter 6).

The Region had no intention of yielding. Despite considerable public pressure and personal attacks on the Head of the Pre-Five Unit, the Region began planning for six community nurseries in 1988/9, though, as it turned out by the end of 1990, only two had materialised.

However, it was never the Regional Council's intention to convert all its existing nurseries overnight:

> While the Member/Officer Group consider the 'community nursery' concept reflects the kind of integrated and flexible service which they would like to see developed, it is the Group's recommendation that the conversion of existing nurseries into 'community nurseries' should be introduced on a gradual progressive basis rather than seeking immediate conversion of all nurseries in Strathclyde. (Strathclyde Regional Council, 1985, p 29)

Concurrent with these developments the Region commissioned an extensive consultation of families with pre-five children. The aim of the survey was to provide a view of the circumstances, priorities and preferences of the consumers of pre-five services. One thousand families were contacted using a one-in-ten sample of all families with children under five, in 29 postcode sectors in Strathclyde Region. One of the main findings from the survey (Penn and Scott, 1989) was that parents expressed a clear preference for flexible local services over an extended form of traditional nursery education, though nursery schooling was the most popular of existing types of provision.

The Region took this finding as vindication for its policy of developing community nurseries and, as stated earlier, two such pilot nurseries were established in 1990: Three Towns Community Nursery in Ayrshire, serving the towns of Saltcoats, Ardrossan and Stevenston and Jigsaw Community Nursery in Dunbartonshire, serving the area of Muirhead and South Strathkelvin.

This highly controversial and ground-breaking initiative by Scotland's largest local authority attracted much attention. An account of the initiative and its development was provided in 1992 by Penn in her book *Under Fives – The View from Strathclyde*, whilst a systematic evaluation of the implementation of the new community nurseries is provided by Wilkinson, Kelly and Stephen (1993). In their report the evaluators found that the community nurseries delivered:

- a nursery environment comparable in quality to that in good nursery schools
- the successful promotion of children's development
- help to many children to overcome anti-social behaviour
- help to many children in stressful family circumstances
- help to many parents to cope better with their children, particularly where relationships had broken down

- the successful targeting of provision at the problems of deprivation
- a significant contribution to preventing children from being taken into care and helping with rehabilitation.

(Wilkinson et al., 1993 p 251)

The evaluators also felt that there was little justification for the vociferous criticism levelled at the concept of community nurseries when it was first launched in 1985. However, this did not mean that all was well with the community nurseries. So much more could have been achieved, particularly if the difficulties with accommodation and staffing had been foreseen. At the end of the first two years the principal weaknesses in relation to the original aims and objectives were deemed to be:

- inadequate provision for under-threes
- inadequate flexibility in the functioning of the nurseries to allow parents to take up opportunities to further their education and training and/or to become more economically active
- insufficient training opportunities for staff, particularly unqualified staff
- insufficient parental and community involvement commensurate with the collective ideals inherent in the term community nursery as expressed in the aims.

(Wilkinson et al., 1993, p 251)

Taking a retrospective view of the community nursery concept and its implementation in Strathclyde, Moss commented:

> ...the community nurseries were only a partial success for a number of reasons, most of which were implicit in the situation in which they were created. The finances were inadequate and irregular, particularly the capital programming. The elongated hierarchy of Strathclyde Region's Education Department meant that, despite the priorities and persuasions of the pre-five unit, the community nurseries were dependent on the erratic goodwill of local administrators for support, advice and progress. (Moss, 1995, p 11)

Although other instances at the local level of integration were taking place, they were also bedevilled by managerial incoherence, to the extent that the co-ordination/integration agenda was left on the back-burner only to be resuscitated in a more vigorous form in 2001 (Scottish Executive, 2001).

Accessibility
Such were the pressures on the Conservative government in the early 1990's to expand early childhood provision that a response was virtually inevitable. Survey after survey (Scott, 1989; Wilkinson et al, 1993) had demonstrated the high demand for pre-school provision. As more and

more mothers were seeking paid employment, the problem of childcare was top priority.

Although places in state-funded nurseries had gradually increased in the early 1990's the increase was starkly insufficient. To meet this demand, a doubling of existing provision would be required at a considerable cost to public funds. Given that the Conservative government in the early 1990's was committed to reducing public expenditure, a vast increase in spending on nursery provision was clearly ruled out. Instead, the government, with a modest layout in expenditure, came up with a scheme — the Voucher Initiative — to expand provision.

> The pre-school Education Voucher Initiative, introduced in England and Wales, and Scotland in 1996, was an important part of the education policy of the then Conservative government. (Stephen et al., 1998, p 1)

The aim of the policy was to expand pre-school education and encourage diversity by allocating parents with a voucher which could be exchanged for a part-time place in pre-school provision. Not only was it an attempt to expand provision: it was also an ideological device to shift more control to parents, away from local authorities — from supplier to consumer.

The initiative was launched as a pilot for the school year 1996–1997 and operated in four local authority areas. An evaluation was undertaken by Stephen et al (1998). In the evaluation the evaluators concluded:

> The introduction of vouchers to change the dynamics of the education market was undoubtedly successful in that it resulted in a larger increase in the supply of pre-school places. (Brown et al., 1998, p 13)

Unfortunately, the initiative failed to promote greater diversity and flexibility in the system. Most of the expansion took place for 4-year olds in the provision of part-time places in nursery classes in primary schools. The traditional half-day, school term arrangement remained intact — but it was perhaps better than nothing.

In retrospect, the voucher scheme commands both admiration and contempt. Brown et al concluded:

> ...we believe that the achievement of an expansion of good quality provision, on the scale we are seeing now and in a very short period of time, required some innovative kindling and an effective spark to get the existing system going. Other means than vouchers could have been used but, in the event, they set pre-school education in Scotland on to a new path. (Brown et al., 1998, p 14)

Quality
The fourth substantive issue in the debate on early childhood services

over the past two decades has been the issue of 'quality'. The debate received a considerable boost with the publication of the Rumbold Report (Department of Education & Science, 1990), which was the *Report of the Committee of Inquiry into the Educational Experience offered to 3- and 4-year old children*. Whilst giving tacit support to the work then taking place in the education of children under 5, it clearly set out the Government's priorities in this field — not one of expansion but one of improving the existing provision:

> Much sound work is going on in the education of children under 5. But we believe that there is a need, made the more urgent by the rapid pace of current change and development within the education system as a whole, to raise the quality of a good deal of existing provision. (DES, 1990, p 1)

Nevertheless, the report generated a consensus in the 1990's in the field of early childhood education that quality matters should be taken seriously. The drive for improvement at national level represented a synthesis of various trends and pressures already gathering momentum. One of the most important of these trends came from the research community, the endeavours of which were focused on finding the features of early childhood provision that best promoted children's development and learning.

Moss and Melhuish (1991), reviewing evidence on a wide range of factors impinging on the day care experience of young children, pointed out that:

> The emphasis now is on gaining understanding, both of theoretical and practical value, of conditions and factors in day care which enhance children's well-being. (Moss and Melhuish, 1991, p 131)

Writing on educational aspects of day care Sylva (1991) stated:

> Overall the evidence for beneficial effects of pre-school experience for three to five year olds on later educational achievement and social adjustment appears to be strong, but the quality of provision will be vital. (Sylva, 1991, p 119)

An important focus in examining 'quality' has been the potential relationship between children's development and children's nursery experience. A study by McCartney (1984) on the effects of the quality of day care on language development demonstrated that language development was poorest in centres which were considered to have a low quality of care (a central feature of the quality measure being the degree of verbal responsiveness). Carew (1980) also found that the responsiveness of caregivers was related to the cognitive and language development of children, with greater responsiveness correlating with enhanced development.

Turning to social development, research again suggested that this was influenced by the quality of education and care offered. One of the first studies was undertaken by Phillips, McCartney and Scarr in 1987. They examined the influence of variations in the quality of childcare provision on children's social development, controlling for other sources of influence such as age, length of experience of a particular childcare environment and family background. They found a relationship between several nursery environmental factors and children's characters in terms of sociability, dependence, aggression, hyperactivity, considerateness and anxiety.

In reviewing the American literature, Clarke-Stewart (1991) identified several indicators of quality that impinge on children's development. These were: a well organised and stimulating physical environment; a responsive and trained care-giver; a balanced curriculum; relatively small groups of children; and relatively generous adult-child ratios. Howes (1991) argued that results from a number of studies suggest that when care-givers demonstrate increased sensitivity, contingency and responsiveness towards children then there are positive affects on developmental patterns. The characteristics of an environment that facilitate this beneficial, responsive style of interaction, she argued, could then be considered indicators of quality.

During the 1990's several studies such as the above were undertaken on the impact on children's development of diverse early years experiences. A useful summary is provided by Stephen, Brown, Cope and Waterhouse (2001). The emphasis in this 'objective' approach to quality has been on exploring the relationship between a range of factors indicative of early childhood educational settings, and various features of children's development and learning:

> It has been assumed that both indicators and outcomes are universal and objective, identifiable through the application of expert knowledge and reliable to accurate measurement given the right technique. (Dahlberg, Moss and Pence, 1999, p 5)

Based on research evidence, the most recent taxonomy of such factors that contribute to a quality early years environment was undertaken by the Childcare Resource & Research Unit in Toronto in 2000. These factors were:

- small group sizes
- high adult : child ratios
- adequate health and safety precautions
- positive ethos
- stable and consistent care
- staff well trained in early childhood education
- decent wages and working conditions

However, an alternative view of 'quality' has been put forward which clearly shows that our understanding of quality in an early years environment is not unproblematic. Such an alternative view, originally outlined by Pence & Moss (1994), represents a challenge to the so-called objective approach prevalent in both the UK and the USA. This challenge has its origins, though not exclusively, in the traditions of early childhood education in Scandinavia, where the subjective experiences of children in complex, pluralistic contexts are seen as central:

> Quality in early childhood services is a constructed concept, subjective in nature and based on values, beliefs and interest, rather than on objective and universal reality. Quality childcare is, to a large extent, in the eye of the beholder. (Pence & Moss, 1994, p 172)

In their book *Beyond Quality in Early Childhood Education*, Dahlberg, Moss and Pence outline the basis of this subjective approach to quality. This approach has:

- identified the importance of the process of defining quality — who is involved and how it is done — and questioned how that process has operated in the past, arguing that it has been dominated by a small group of experts, to the exclusion of a wide range of other stakeholders with an interest in early childhood institutions;
- understood quality to be a subjective, value-based, relative and dynamic concept, with the possibility of multiple perspectives or understandings of what quality is;
- argued that work with quality needs to be contextualized, spatially and temporally, and to recognize cultural and other significant forms of diversity.

(Dahlberg, Moss and Pence, 1999, p 5)

Assuming one is convinced of the arguments in support of the subjective approach, applying it in practice is not straightforward. It implies that what takes place in an early years setting is embedded in the process of negotiation between different stakeholder groups — professionals, parents, funders and, not least, children themselves. It would be difficult to accept that all such stakeholders did not accept that a quality early years environment should work in children's best interests, in other words, serve to optimise the opportunities for promoting learning and development.

Although strong evidence exists to support the view that a high quality nursery environment has a positive and substantial impact on learning and development in 3- and 4- year old children, there is concern about the impact of non-maternal care on younger children, particularly in the first year of life.

> …appreciation is growing that child-care quality may not have as substantial an impact on child development as was often presumed was the case. (Belsky, 2001, p 855)

Much of this concern has arisen from a large-scale, longitudinal study conducted in the US, undertaken by the National Institute of Child Health and Human Development (NICHD). The findings from this study (NICHD, 2001) suggest that as the quantity of non-maternal care increased so did children's neediness (for example, demands for attention and immediacy), assertiveness (for example, excessive talking and argument), disobedience and aggression (See Chapter 6).

But children themselves are not the only group to be considered in the 'quality' debate. Quite rightly, Balageur, Mestres and Penn (1992) identified two further perspectives when considering quality: parents and professionals. To quote from Balageur et al:

> Parents are not a homogeneous group. Although they may have common interests, they are as individual as their children. A parent may have different criteria from professionals. For example, she may consider maintaining family income as a priority for family stability and therefore seek daycare — whereas professionals may argue that other forms of care are more appropriate for her child. Parents from a black community may feel strongly that white professionals do not fully understand the pressures and oppressions that their children experience. A parent might have a decided view about gender — about the right way to bring up boys and girls — which conflicts with professional opinion. There may be differences about discipline and if and how children should be punished. Professionals sometimes argue that by virtue of their training and experience they have the best interests of the child at heart, and are in a better position to judge than parents what is best. (Balageur et al., 1992, p 6)

Pressure for improvement in services was also brought to bear by the European Commission Network on Childcare (ECNC) at national level in all European countries. The Commission published a discussion paper in 1992 by Balaguer et al. *Quality in Services for Young Children.* Drawing on diverse views and perspectives from different European countries, the paper posed two important questions: How should we define good quality? and, What conditions are necessary to promote good quality services? The response to those questions was embedded in the Network's approach to quality:

- quality is a relative concept, based on values and beliefs
- defining quality is a process and this process is important in its own right, providing opportunities to share, discuss and understand values, ideas, knowledge and experience
- the process should be participatory and democratic, involving different groups, including children, parents and families and professionals working in services

- the needs, perspectives and values of these groups may sometimes differ
- defining quality should be seen as a dynamic and continuous process, involving regular review and never reaching a final, 'objective' statement.

> (European Commission Network on Childcare, 1996, p 7)

On the basis of the above assumptions, the paper proposed a framework for promoting better quality services. It was followed two years later by a second report — *Quality in Services for Young Children* (ECNC, 1996). In this report 40 targets were identified. The report concluded:

> Reaching these targets would not be the end of the search for quality; that is a dynamic and continuous process, involving regular reflection and review. But reaching the targets would go a long way towards assuring equal access to good quality services for all young children in the European Union. (European Commission Network on Childcare, 1996, p 32)

A further area of concern in the quality debate focused on the tension between promoting quality and monitoring quality. Both Clarke-Stewart (1991) and Harms, Clifford and Cryer (1998) have argued in favour of setting and monitoring minimum standards as indicators of quality, whereas, on the other hand, Balageur et al (1992) have argued in favour of promoting quality:

> Our broader aim is to engender discussion and provide a focus for debating high quality services, to look at what we might try to achieve to put our beliefs and our values about children into practice. (Balageur et al., 1992, p 8)

The pressures on public institutions in the early 1990's, however, to demonstrate they were providing value-for-money meant that an emphasis on quality assurance emerged. In 1995 the HM Inspectors of Schools published an extensive manual *Using Performance Indicators in Nursery School/Class/Pre-Five Unit Self Evaluation* (SOED, 1995), specifying how early education settings should monitor their activities.

Quality assurance played a central role in the process. But the drive for quality assurance was not restricted to the local authority sector. Both the independent sector and the voluntary sector put in train mechanisms to develop their own quality assurance schemes. In 1997 the Scottish Pre-school Play Association published its quality assurance scheme for sessional playgroups (SPPA, 1997). In the independent sector a scheme was developed for the Scottish Independent Nurseries Association (SINA) by Stephen and Wilkinson and launched in 1996 with considerable enthusiasm. In an evaluation of the scheme based on private nurseries which belonged to SINA it was found that:

- nearly all the nurseries provide a stimulating and caring environment for babies and young children
- all nurseries communicate effectively with parents
- most have a curricular framework in place
- most have an assessment/record-keeping policy
- many nurseries employed a range of staff, including teachers and nursery nurses
- many have a staff appraisal scheme and staff development opportunities
- some have a very effective equal opportunities policy

(Wilkinson and Stephen, 1998, p 35)

Nevertheless, it was also found that:

with one exception, all SINA nurseries were lacking a modern, systematic approach to their planning and co-ordination of children's learning activities. All the nurseries were advised to put in place a clear and visible relationship between the nursery's aims, the curricular areas, the learning outcomes, the learning activities and the record-keeping practices. (Wilkinson & Stephen, 1998, p 35)

However, for those private nurseries outwith SINA considerable concern has been expressed about the quality of provision in such nurseries (Glasgow Herald, 4.10.02), a matter which the new Scottish Executive would take up in its Childcare Strategy.

CHAPTER 2

THE NEW AGENDA

2.1 Introduction

In May 1997, a new Labour government was elected, the first Labour government in the UK for 18 years. This signalled the start of a radically different approach to education and early childhood education in particular. Overnight, early childhood education and care were transformed from being the 'Cinderella' to the 'Jewel in the Crown' in the education systems of the UK.

For those who work in early childhood education the realm of politics, ideology and governance may seem at best irrelevant, at worst, a distraction. The day-to-day tasks of educating and caring for young children, on the face of it, seem remote from the affairs of governments. Admittedly, until the 1990's, early childhood education and care were not the central concern of either Conservative or Labour governments. Not surprisingly, therefore, professional perspectives on early education virtually ignored the contemporary social policy debates. In more recent times this position is untenable. Since 1997 the state has adopted a more powerful stance on educational and social issues, a stance that has profound implications for our work with families and young children. The two Labour Governments post 1997, and recently the Scottish Executive, have issued a raft of policies that have major significance for those who work with young children.

Given that the Labour Party adopted the slogan 'Education, Education, Education' in its election campaign, it wasted little time in setting out its proposals. In November 1997 a Consultation Paper was published — *Education in Early Childhood: the Pre-School Years* (SOEID, 1997b). In his Foreword to the Consultation Paper, the then Minister for Education & Industry in Scotland, Brian Wilson, stated:

> Education is the Government's number one priority. And in Education nothing is more important than the opportunities we give our youngest children in the years before primary school. (Wilson, 1997, p i)

The Government's early years agenda as set out in this Consultation Paper was extensive and ambitious. The issues identified in Chapter 1 were central to this agenda. On the issue of *accessibility*, the Government committed itself to offering by the winter of 1998–99 a quality part-time educational place to all children in their pre-school year, i.e. to all 4-year olds. It also recognised that places for children in their ante- pre-school year (that is, 3-year olds) should also be offered a place as resources became available. To realise this very ambitious expansion the Government endorsed the 'mixed-economy' model of provision which involves the public sector, the voluntary sector and the independent sector. To do this required the exploration of new routes to partnership.

> All providers, whether local authorities or the private and voluntary sectors, have much to learn from each other, and the government is happy to encourage this process. (SOEID, 1997b, p 11)

On the issue of *quality*, the Paper recognised the critical importance of this issue in its expansion programme: *the quality of those places needs to be maintained and enhanced, broadened and deepened.* It was proposed that the approach to quality assurance in the public, private and voluntary sectors should be based on a combination of self-evaluation, guidance and support from the local authority, and inspection by HM inspectors. On *co-ordination/integration*, the Paper recognised the need to develop more integrated services in the early years:

> And part-time education to satisfy children's appetite for learning has to be integrated with services to meet their other important needs for companionship, comfort and health, and their families' needs for support. (SOEID, 1997b, p 39)

On the matter of *curriculum*, the Paper endorsed the *Curriculum Framework* which had been introduced by the previous Conservative administration. It recognised the importance of having available to all pre-school centres in Scotland a clear statement of the range of learning experiences which should be available to all children in the pre-school year: *an authoritative statement which will be available to all* (SOEID, 1997b, p 24). Furthermore, in the Consultation Paper the government undertook to issue a new draft of the Curriculum Framework which would be more broadly focused, and address the needs of children over two pre-school years rather than one.

By any standard, the government was proposing in its Consultation Paper a major sea-change in the provision of education and care for families with young children in Scotland. This sea-change could not be realised without a very considerable investment of public funds. But on what grounds could such a large injection of public funds be justified?

2.2 Governance

The justification for the Labour Government's policies, not only in education, but in all other areas of government, was based on what Giddens

(1998) referred to as *The Third Way*. The 'New Labour' Prime Minister, Tony Blair, was particularly impressed by this new approach to social democracy as a basis for his Government's reform programme:

> Reform of the state and government should be a basic orientating principle of third way politics — a process of the deepening and widening of democracy. (Giddens, 1998, p 69)

But the very title *The Third Way* assumes that two different and opposing ideologies preceded it. To understand the basis of the new social democracy and its impact on early childhood education, it is worthwhile briefly reviewing the salient features of these opposing ideologies.

Opposing ideologies
Two ideologies that have underpinned political thinking in Britain, particularly since 1945, are neo-liberalism (sometimes referred to as classical liberalism or the New Right) and socialism (referred to as old-style social democracy or the Old Left). In addition to other major differences, they are diametrically opposed to each other on the role of the state in both public and private affairs. For neo-liberalism, as enshrined in the New Right of the Conservative governments between 1979 and 1997, the state, if expanded too far, becomes the enemy of freedom and self-reliance:

> The state, particularly the welfare state, is said to be destructive of the civil order, but markets are not, because they thrive on individual initiative. (Giddens, 1998, p 12)

According to Eccleshall et al., neo-liberalism or classical liberalism by which it is sometimes known:

> views society as a collection of independent individuals, and wishes to curtail government activity in social and economic matters. (Eccleshall et al., 1984, p 89)

It follows, therefore, according to this view, that the overall well-being of society is generated by unregulated competition. It was assumed that a 'free' society fosters self-discipline and thus strengthens the moral fibre of its citizens. It was this kind of thinking that promoted competition in education in the 1980's and 1990's as a means of raising standards. This minimalist role for government in social affairs, such as the care and nurture of young children, explains the reluctance of successive Conservative governments post-1979 to invest more resources into welfare policies:

> The welfare state is seen as the source of all evils in much the same way capitalism once was by the revolutionary left. (Giddens, 1998, p 13)

Welfare was regarded as a safety net for families unable to cope, not as a necessary support for the onerous but rewarding task of bringing up and educating young children. Such matters were seen as the prime responsibility of parents: the state only intervened when something went drastically wrong.

It is hardly surprising, therefore, to understand why the Conservative governments of the 1980's were reluctant to expand public provision for the education and care of young children, despite the fact that it was a Conservative government in 1972 that promised nursery education for all! Even the Voucher Scheme (see Chapter 1) was fundamentally 'the sprat to catch the mackerel' in the sense that the scheme was expected to encourage individual families to use their own resources to top-up the value of the voucher and to access what the parents regarded as the most appropriate provision for their children in the independent and voluntary sectors as well as in the public sector. In this respect, the voucher initiative was a miserable failure, despite its effect of creating more provision (see Stephen et al., 1998). Advocates of the scheme will no doubt take the view that the scheme was not given sufficient time to become fully operational. There is little doubt that, in the future, such initiatives will be resuscitated, given the emerging position on the Right for more 'consumer' control over public services.

But what of socialism or the old-style social democracy? At the centre of such an ideology was the principle of wealth re-distribution to overcome inequality. To undertake such a re-distribution would require powerful state intervention, not only in economic matters but also in other matters such as education and welfare. Socialism required a comprehensive welfare state to 'protect' citizens from the harsh realities of inequality from 'cradle to grave' generated by the capitalist system characteristic of western democracies.

An example of such protection was the introduction of the National Health Service by the Labour Government elected in 1945. In education, it was a Labour Government that brought in comprehensive schooling in 1965, in response to the inequalities reinforced by selecting children at age 11 on the basis of 'ability' for a particular type of secondary school — the academy or the junior secondary school. On family matters, the Labour Government of 1997–2001 introduced the Families' Working Tax Credit (see Chapter 3) to help families shoulder the cost of early childhood education and care. It was therefore justified for the state to engage in supporting critical social processes such as family life.

> For classical social democracy, government involvement in family life is necessary and to be applauded. State benefits are vital for rescuing families in need, and the state should step in wherever individuals, for one reason or another, are unable to fend for themselves. (Giddens, 1998, p 9)

The response of all governments since 1945 to family matters has always been controversial. Since 1945 the family as an institution has experienced a metamorphosis — from the 'extended' family of the pre- and immediate post-war period, to the 'nuclear' family of the 1960's, to the 'pluralist' family of the 1990's and the new millennium. It would be difficult for governments to be oblivious to such fundamental changes. Rather than adopt a laissez-faire approach characteristic of the New Right, the new style social democracy advocates a more proactive approach based on engagement and inclusion.

But expansion of the Welfare State, it has been argued, led to perverse consequences — an over-dependency of individuals on state handouts, decaying, crime-ridden housing estates and parents often neglecting their family responsibilities. To the new Labour Government this was not the route to a fairer, decent and more open society. As an alternative, the Labour Government turned to a new form of social democracy — *The Third Way*.

2.3 The Third Way

As indicated earlier in this chapter, the basis for the present Government's policies is what is often referred at *The Third Way*. This new social democracy purports a number of axioms which serve as the bedrock of the ideology. In summary, these are:

- equality (in terms of equality of opportunity)
- protection of the vulnerable
- freedom as autonomy
- no rights without responsibilities
- no authority without democracy
- promotion of pluralism
- modernisation

This is a formidable list of axioms which now permeate the provision of all public services in the UK.

It is claimed by Giddens (1998) that the overall aim of third way politics should be to *help citizens pilot their way through the major revolutions of our time: globalisation, transformations in personal life and our relationship to nature*. To achieve this aim, Giddens has put forward the notion of the Social Investment State. In such a state, education is pivotal:

> Governments need to emphasize *life-long education*, developing education programmes that start from an individual's early years and continue on late in life. Although training in specific skills may be necessary for many job transitions, more important is the development of cognitive and emotional competence. Instead of relying on un-conditional benefits, policies should be oriented to encourage saving, the use of educational resources and other personal investment opportunities. (Giddens, 1998, p 125)

Not only does Giddens locate education, and early years education in particular, in a process of lifelong learning, he also emphasises the need for more competent citizens — competent in their cognitive and emotional living. The foundation for this competence is to be found in the family and in early childhood education, not as separate entities but working in close partnership for a better society. To quote Giddens again:

> Sustaining continuity in family life, especially protecting the well-being of children, is one of the most important goals of family policy. This can't be achieved, however, through a reactionary stance, an attempt to reinstate the 'traditional family'. (Giddens, 1998, p 68)

In its task of translating the fundamental values of the new social democracy, the Labour Government has been faced with a number of apparent contradictions:

> Modernising social democrats have to find an approach that reconciles equality with pluralism and life-style diversity, whilst recognising that the clashes between freedom and equality to which classical liberals have always pointed are real. (Giddens, 10th ESRC Lecture, October 1999)

The publication of the Government's childcare strategy in 1998 was an attempt to find a way through some of these contradictions in the interests of families and young children (see Chapter 4).

2.4 Critics of the Third Way

Critics of the Third Way are primarily located in the macro-political arena rather than being concerned with matters pertaining to the way in which children are socialised and educated.

In an attempt to summarise the criticisms and to construct a response, Giddens (2000) categorised them into six areas. The first concerns criticisms levelled at the ideological basis of Third Way politics. Such a basis is seen by the critics as ill-defined and opaque. Attempts at coherence are regarded as fundamentally negative as they are based on the perceived shortcomings of either the New Right, or the old social democracy. The second criticism is focused on the location of Third Way politics. Is it Centre-Left or Centre-Right? The Third Way is often confused with more conservative positions and policies and such confusion has been expressed in colloquial terms — 'Blair is like Thatcher without the handbag'. The fact that the Third Way does not overtly and unequivocally enshrine the traditional egalitarianism of the Old Left makes it vulnerable to this criticism. Thirdly, the Third Way is criticised for embracing the capitalist ethic by failing to contest the inequalities of income, wealth and power endemic in British society, a criticism commonly levelled at liberalism. Fourthly, the Third Way is criticised for saying nothing new to the modern world. British society already has a well developed welfare system in which the state readily accepts responsibility for the more vulnerable members of our society. The relevance for Britain of Third Way politics is therefore seen by some as peripheral. Fifthly, the ideology is criticised for having no distinctive economic policy other than that dictated by capitalism. It is therefore vulnerable to forces at work in the market place with no plan to act as a buttress to any future major economic downturn. Finally, it is criticised for not addressing sufficiently robustly the ecological crisis in which the world at large now finds itself. Clearly these criticisms are formidable and any systematic response is beyond the scope of this book. Several of the criticisms however impinge on the relationship between the state and the family.

Whilst these criticisms do not address directly the role of education, the alleged obfuscation surrounding Third Way philosophy fuels uncertainly regarding other aspects of the philosophy more concerned with families and young children. Third Way politicians seem to defend the family — even the traditional construction of the family — as a means of providing the primary socialisation for children and consequently the control of anti-social behaviour in children. Emphasis is also placed on personal, individual responsibility for such behaviour, rather than the conditions under which anti-social behaviour is fostered. Many would argue that such thinking is more aligned with conservative perspectives than those of the Centre-Left. One matter, however, is certain: ideological considerations of the family and its role in contemporary society are crucial to determining the use of public funds for early childhood education and care. To date, this ideological debate has been polarised in terms of Left and Right politics.

According to Muncie et al. (1995) *The Conservative party has long claimed that it is the true party of the family* where the emphasis is on the traditional structural arrangements, i.e. stable marriage between the adults. Functionally such families are considered to be more natural and superior to any other form, for example, the lone-parent family, in their task of socialising and disciplining children. In addition, they are relatively autonomous of the state, thus cultivating a sense of ownership of the children in the family by the parents. Other family structures are often blamed by members of the New Right for promoting moral degradation, delinquency and under-achievement. Even the idea of working mothers in a stable marriage relationship where there are children presents an irritating paradox for the New Right. Whilst it recognises that many women make an invaluable contribution to the economic well-being of society, their primary purpose, at least before children start formal school at 5 years of age, is to be the all-ready, all-available mainstay of domestic efficiency. Such thinking is diametrically opposed to feminist ideas about equality and the identity of women (New and David, 1985).

On the other hand, social democratic ideology regards the family as a *social institution* with reciprocal responsibilities for the parents and the state. In other words, children are not 'owned' entirely by their parents. The state has the responsibility of supporting the adult members in the family to fulfil their functions effectively. Structural considerations, for example, marriage, are considered to be less important. Of crucial significance however are the relationships inside the family, where warmth, love, support and caring are paramount. In order for such values to flourish in contemporary families, the state has a moral obligation to become involved, especially when the family becomes vulnerable to external pressures. But the social democratic state has a responsibility to all families, not just those that are vulnerable. The provision of childcare and other services such as counselling and conciliation are central. Given the emphasis of Third Way philosophy on the celebration of diversity, it is appropriate to ask: how different does diversity have to be before celebration turns to despair?

As indicated in a later chapter, family life in the UK has changed so much over the past decade that there can be no turning back to the traditional family as the unitary arrangement for bringing up children. The most significant question to be asked is *How can the State best support all families to ensure that children are loved and cared for and have a sense of right or wrong?* Such is the concern of Third Way politics on matters pertaining to the family. Generating and implementing fair social policies to facilitate the optimisation of opportunities is a feature of New Labour. Unfortunately, just as the New Right faces a paradox with its social policy on the family, so does New Labour. On the one hand, whilst recognising that promoting and maintaining the quality of relationships inside the family is at the core, acceptance of liberty and space for individuals within relativistic diverse family structures does not necessarily promote such relationships. The work of McLanahan and Sandetur (1994) demonstrated that children brought up in lone-parent families tend, but not always, to be worse off than children brought up in a family with both biological parents — and not just in a material sense. Often lone-parent families fell short of meeting the social and emotional needs of their children.

It is claimed by Third Way sympathisers that the duality between Left and Right in family policy — between those who celebrate diversity and those who advocate tradition — has been unfruitful. Wilkinson (1998) points out that:

> Problems being experienced by families today are rooted both in economic stress (whether of time or money) and in family disintegration. Any progressive family policy must address both these issues or it will fail. (Wilkinson, 1998, p 12)

Addressing economic stress, particularly stress concerned with childcare provision, has been taken up by the new Labour Government (see chapter 3). However, addressing family disintegration is much more complex.

Whilst a progressive family policy can help to support families and help shoulder the burden of bringing up children, it cannot have any direct impact on the relationship between the adults in the family. Women, including married women, with children, are becoming increasingly empowered. The majority of employees in a wide range of caring and caring-linked professions — education, health, social work, psychological services — are now female. Inevitably, such empowerment impacts on the male-female relationships, with many men unable to adapt to their increasingly uncertain role. As yet there has been no parallel men's movement akin to the women's movement of the 1960's and 1970's, perhaps because the sense of frustration felt by many women at that time was positively outwardly focused, whereas in contemporary times men channel their frustrations inwardly and more negatively. A family policy for the new millennium must find ways of re-engaging fathers with the caring process. It is not sufficient for any family policy to take a laissez-faire approach to family disintegration in the name of diversity. As Giddens put it:

> (Governments)... should foster conditions in which individuals are able to form stable ties with others, especially where children are involved and accept responsibilities that come along with contemporary freedoms. (Giddens, 2000, p 47)

An essential feature of these 'conditions' to which Giddens refers is the provision of a high quality early childhood education and care for all families who wish it. The next chapter will outline how the Scottish Executive intends to achieve this.

CHAPTER 3

THE NEW STRATEGY FOR CHILDCARE IN SCOTLAND

3.1 Introduction

This Government was elected to build a modern Britain and a fair and decent society, but they are under pressure. Women and men struggle with choices over work and family responsibilities, whether to stay at home with their children full-time or balance home responsibilities with work. The Government is pledged to support families and children. But we must do so in new ways which reflect the new challenges which they face. (Blair, 1998, p v)

In our election manifesto we undertook to produce a childcare strategy for Scotland which would 'match the requirements of a modern labour market and enable parents, especially women, to balance family and working life....' This Green Paper marks a major step forward in meeting that commitment. It makes clear our intention to bring about a step change in the provision of childcare for Scotland. (Dewar, 1998, p vii)

These two statements — first by the Prime Minister and the second by the Secretary of State for Scotland — are an historic landmark in early education and care in Scotland. They appear in the opening pages to the Government's Consultation Paper, *Meeting the Childcare Challenge — A Childcare Strategy for Scotland* (The Scottish Office, 1998). This Consultation Paper represented what many commentators had been seeking for some considerable time, that is, a comprehensive statement of intent for early childhood education and care based on an understanding of contemporary social issues, backed with the necessary resources. The paper identified three major issues to be addressed: the variable quality in current services, the high cost of some services and the poor availability of services in many areas. In addressing these issues the *Childcare Strategy for Scotland* put forward three steps:

- Raising the quality of care

- Making childcare more affordable and
- Making childcare more accessible by increasing places and improving information.

(The Scottish Office, 1998a, p xi)

The Consultation Paper articulated five principles on which the strategy is based: quality, affordability, diversity, accessibility, and partnership.

These principles are firmly aligned with *Third Way* policies as addressed in Chapter 2 and form part of the Government's drive for social inclusion.

3.2 The 'Quality' Strategy

The Consultation Paper set out the Government's agenda for improving quality in the delivery of early childhood services in Scotland:

- improving *regulation*, including work on developing a better system for day care and early education inspection.
- encouraging the adoption of *quality assurance* arrangements, including integrating childcare and learning where appropriate.
- establishing an *Early Excellence in Practice* initiative to demonstrate the highest standards in early education and child-care provision and disseminating *good practice*.
- boosting the *recruitment and supply* of competent people to work with children, in particular by raising the standards, status and attractiveness of childcare and playwork as an occupation.
- *setting standards* in the training, skills and qualifications of childcare and playwork staff and establishing a clear, comprehensive *qualifications and careers structure*.

(The Scottish Office, 1998a, p 7)

In 1998, the legal requirements for the **regulation** of formal childcare in the private and voluntary sectors were based on the Children Act 1989. Such regulation assured minimum standards in terms of fitness of carers, their qualifications, adult : child ratios and the physical environment. These requirements were often augmented by quality assurance schemes developed independently by the Scottish Pre-school Play Association (SPPA, 1997) and the Scottish Independent Nurseries Association (Stephen and Wilkinson, 1996). However, a number of anomalies were recognised in the current regulation arrangements: for example, minimum staffing ratios were enforced for playgroups, childminders and private nurseries but not for nursery schools and classes catering for children of the same age. Unfairness in the system was very apparent.

Following the publication of *Childcare Strategy*, the Scottish Office rapidly developed new proposals for the *Regulation of Early Education and Childcare* in the form of a Consultation Paper (The Scottish Office,

1999b). The Paper addressed the role and requirements of regulation against three key aims:

- ensuring children's safety
- ensuring that children's experience in early education and childcare promotes their personal and social development as well as being enjoyable and stimulating
- ensuring that the regulatory burden is not disproportionate and that provision of similar types is subject to similar regulation

(The Scottish Office, 1999b, p 6)

In its White Paper *Targeting Excellence* the Government proposed the setting up of a new regulatory body for all establishments providing care in Scotland, to be called the *Scottish Commission for the Regulation of Care* (see Chapter 6). It was intended that this new Commission would have responsibility for registration, inspection and associated activities in a wide range of care settings. It was not surprising to learn therefore that the Consultation Paper on regulation subsequently proposed to allocate the responsibility for the regulation of childcare to this new Commission. Undoubtedly, this proposal was a milestone in the development of early childhood services in Scotland. The Paper outlined the substantive issues for consultation: what to regulate; how to regulate; and the standards to be achieved. Twenty-nine questions on these matters were contained in the Paper.

Following wide consultation, the new Scottish Executive published its response in *Regulation of Early Education and Childcare – The Way Ahead* (Scottish Executive, 2000b). The idea of the new Commission was adopted with widespread support from those working in the field. But such a major innovation required appropriate legislation to be brought before the new Scottish Parliament. The Regulation of Care (Scotland) Act was passed in 2001. Shortly afterwards, new national care standards for childcare services for children and young people up to the age of 16 were published (see Chapter 6).

Turning to the matter of **quality assurance** for nursery schools and classes in the public sector, quality assurance has traditionally been addressed through HMI inspections, albeit at infrequent intervals, that is, approximately every six years. Since 1997 such inspections were largely based on the *Curriculum Framework for Children in their Pre-school Year* and augmented by the report *Using Performance Indicators in Nursery School/Class/Pre-Five Unit Self Evaluation* (SOED, 1995).

In the Childcare Strategy document it was recognised that a more consistent approach to quality assurance was required:

> There is now a need to explore in more detail the output quality standards for day care and early education, to reflect the interdependence of these services for young children. We need to do so in a way that

will help the pre-school centres benchmark their own performance, and help practitioners recognise and promote characteristics of quality provision. (The Scottish Office, 1998a, p 9)

Following this statement of intent in 1998, the new Scottish Executive, the policy-making arm of the recently re-established Scottish Parliament, commissioned a self-evaluation guide for all early years settings. *The Child at the Centre* was published by the Executive in 1999.

The specific aim of this guide is to provide the benchmark of quality provision in the early years sector. We recognise that others have worked to develop self-evaluation guides and these will help to ensure high quality. (Galbraith, 1999, p 3)

In tandem with this guide, the Childcare Strategy Consultation Paper also encouraged the independent and voluntary sectors to put in place *proper arrangements for quality assurance*. The scheme developed by the Scottish Independent Nurseries Association was recognised in the Strategy document:

The Scottish Independent Nurseries Association has developed a very comprehensive quality assurance scheme for its members. It covers the whole range of key areas important to running a nursery such as the learning environment and social experience offered to children, management, staffing and accommodation. Particular emphasis is placed on partnership with parents, the local authority and others. (The Scottish Office, 1998a, p 9)

In addition to *The Child at the Centre*, and the recognition of quality assurance schemes, the Government, through the work of the Scottish Consultative Committee on the Curriculum (SCCC), has also put in place national curriculum guidelines for children aged 3–5 which are an extension of the guidelines previously published:

The curriculum framework is based on the fundamental principle of equality of opportunity. All education systems of quality must recognise that no individual or group should be disadvantaged on the grounds of race, gender, culture, disability, class, belief, lifestyle or family circumstances. Effective learning and teaching can only take place in an atmosphere of mutual trust, respect and security. An inclusive approach is therefore essential to the provision of high quality learning experiences for all children. (The Scottish Office, 1999a, p iii)

As with the previous version for children in their pre-school year, the new Curriculum Framework was warmly welcomed. The Framework document (The Scottish Office, 1999a) endorsed the fundamental features of a child-centred approach but at the same time outlined what forms of learning many practitioners feel is appropriate for young children in the modern world.

The original five key aspects of children's development and learning were seen as vital in the guidelines, with children's *emotional, personal and social development* given pride of place:

> The importance of emotional, personal and social development cannot be over-emphasised, particularly for the youngest children. For them, arrival in new and strange places can be an anxious and unsettling experience. They should be supported by providing a clear settling-in period with familiar routines and lots of support for both the child and the parent. (The Scottish Office, 1999a, p 9)

Recent work by Golman (1997, 2000) on *Emotional Intelligence* has underlined the fact that for children to be successful both in their subsequent schooling and in later life they must be able to use their meta-cognitive capacities to reflect on and understand not only their emotional response to situations encountered but also the feelings of others in response to others' behaviour. It is fitting therefore that the Guidelines recognise the need for professionals working with young children to facilitate children's emotional development.

Children also need to feel a sense of security, especially when, in modern times, many children are affected by upheaval in family circumstances. Early childhood education services are in a unique position to help children deal with turmoil. Often, when children start nursery or playgroup, they display social, emotional and developmental problems, even such anti-social behaviour as biting and scratching other children. Given stability in the nursery environment and sensitive and responsive staff, very considerable inroads can be made into helping such children deal with their difficulties (Kelly, 1995).

Not all children, by any means, have experienced difficult situations before they start nursery or playgroup. For the vast majority of children nursery is a natural extension of the home environment. But it is also a time when their world can be perplexing — new friendships, new choices, new demands, new tensions and new routines are commonplace. Addressing these matters helps children to grow emotionally. The Curriculum Framework gives recognition to this development and by encouraging children to:

- develop confidence, self-esteem and a sense of security
- care for themselves and their personal safety
- develop independence, for example in dressing and personal hygiene
- persevere in tasks that at first present some difficulties
- express appropriately feelings, needs and preferences
- form positive relationships with other children and adults, and begin to develop particular friendships with other children

- become aware of and respect the needs and feelings of others in their behaviour, and learn to follow rules
- make and express choices, plans and decisions
- play co-operatively, take turns and share resources
- become aware that the celebration of cultural and religious festivals is important in people's lives
- develop positive attitudes towards others whose gender, language, religion or culture, for example, is different from their own
- care for the environment and for other people in the community

(The Scottish Office, 1999a, p 9)

In the early years an emphasis on supporting children in their social, emotional and personal development is paramount:

> If nurseries are encouraged to foster children's personal, social and human qualities they are surely opening doors for them to live a life of personal fulfilment whatever their achievements. (Dowling, 2000, p xxiv)

In her book, Dowling (2000) uses a range of case studies to help early years professionals and parents to translate contemporary theories into sound practice. She endorses the view that:

> It is not what we are born with that counts so much but what we are allowed to do and who we are encouraged to be. (Dowling, 2000, p 1)

Encouragement, freedom with responsibility and awareness are the basic values on which best practice in early childhood education is founded. Unfortunately, many children are denied access to environments that cherish such values. All too often family environments can have a constraining and sometimes a catastrophic effect on children's well-being, albeit inadvertently, though often as a consequence of their family's situation. It is vital therefore that early years professionals work in partnership with parents in children's best interests.

Other aspects of children's development and learning are also important, none more so than children's *communication and language*.

> The development of children's skills in language is central to their abilities to communicate in relationships and learning, to understand ideas and to order, explore and refine their thoughts. (The Scottish Office, 1999a, p 15)

As with all other areas of children's development, adults play a vital role in the development of children's language development. Not only are they able to provide good role models by listening to and talking with children, they can encourage children who for one reason or another seem unwilling to express themselves in a public domain.

In the *Knowledge and Understanding of the World* section of the

Curriculum Framework the 'child-centred' approach to the curriculum is continued. At the core of this section is the enhancement of children's awareness of the world around them by giving expression to their natural curiosity. Clearly this is a vast domain, from awareness of their immediate material world to awareness of their environment — both physical and social. Perhaps it is here that the role of the professional — nursery nurse, nursery teacher or playleader — is somewhat controversial. Should the professional instil knowledge of an instrumental kind, for example, word recognition, simple arithmetical operations, etc., often referred to in its extreme forms as the technicist agenda, or should the knowledge emerge from children's own day-to-day experiences — the progressivist agenda? The balance between the two is crucial, as it brings into play how the professionals use their authority.

The fourth area of the curriculum is concerned with children's *experience and aesthetic development*. In this domain the Curriculum Framework specifies that children should learn to:

• investigate and use a variety of media and techniques such as painting, drawing, printing and modelling with fabrics, clay and other materials
• express thoughts and feelings in pictures, paintings and models
• use role play or puppets to recreate and invent situations
• use verbal and non-verbal language in role play
• listen and respond to sounds, rhythms, songs and a variety of music
• make music by singing, clapping and playing percussion instruments
• use instruments by themselves and in groups to invent music that expressed their thoughts and feelings
• move rhythmically and expressively to music
• participate in simple dances and singing games

(The Scottish Office, 1999a, p 32)

There is a growing body of evidence that suggests that the development of children's expressive abilities, for example, in musical expression, has a knock-on effect on children's response to other learning situations. As with *emotional, personal and social development* the underlying feature is the concept of emotional intelligence (Golman, 1997), which not only enables children to become more aware of both themselves and others but enables them to 'manage' themselves and others better.

A curriculum would not be comprehensive if it did not include children's *physical development and movement*. In this domain children are encouraged to:

• enjoy energetic activity both indoors and out and the feeling of well being that it brings
• explore different ways in which they can use their bodies in physical activity

- use their bodies to express ideas and feelings in response to music and imaginative ideas
- run, jump, skip, climb, balance, throw and catch with increasing skill and confidence
- co-operate with others in physical play and games
- develop increasing control of the fine movements of their fingers and hands
- develop an awareness of space
- be safe in movement and in using tools and equipment
- be aware of the importance of health and fitness

(The Scottish Office, 1999a, p 37)

With rising levels of obesity in children in several western countries, attention to health and fitness promotion is becoming more important. Children need access to varied opportunities to engage in physical exercise more and more.

Reflecting on these curriculum developments, it would not be unreasonable to feel somewhat uneasy at the incursion of the state into an area of education traditionally left to trained professionals and parents. Centralisation inevitably leads to greater control, with the possible consequences of greater conformity and uniformity. A critical issue in this debate is whether this enhanced centralisation provides sufficient scope for individuality to flourish or whether centralisation inadvertently operates to crush curiosity. Such individuality is usually expressed through choices and spontaneity. For young children the medium for such 'choice and spontaneity' is their play activity. Play is a central feature of young children's behaviour for a whole spectrum of reasons. Fortunately, the new Curriculum Framework gives some recognition to this, but perhaps not enough.

To support all these developments and disseminate them throughout Scotland, the Executive put in place the *Best Practice Initiative*. This national initiative organised seminars and conferences throughout Scotland for professionals working in the field of early childhood education and care. A newsletter was also widely distributed.

However, of critical importance in delivering the Childcare's Strategy is the professional competence of childcare workers — essentially, nursery nurses, nursery teachers and play-leaders and others. The Government's 1997 consultation paper *Education in Early Childhood: The Pre-School Years* (SOED, 1997b) highlighted the range of qualifications available in early childhood education and care with different conditions of service attached. The Childcare Strategy document proposed a setting up of a *clear, comprehensive framework of qualifications across the whole early years and childcare sector*. The Government's intention was to:

Support the Scottish Qualifications Authority and the emerging
network of National Training Organisations in developing the
"climbing frame" of training and qualifications. They will map
existing training, qualifications and the various childcare-related
occupations. (The Scottish Office, 1998a, p 14)

But professional input to young children's development and learning is
not by itself sufficient. The most important ingredient is the parent. If
parents do not give time to children and set them good role models, the
effectiveness of the professional is severely limited. Perhaps the most
important challenge facing us all is how to promote more responsible
parenting, not just in the early years but throughout a child's education.

In her book Watt (1990) makes a link between parenting skills and the
vulnerabilities experienced by many families. For children's well-being
— both short- and long-term — it is vital that children receive warm,
loving and consistent support from parents. If a parent is in a vulnerable
situation — and all too many are — then the relationship with the child
can be seriously impaired, with the possibility of long-term mental health
problems. In the research on community nurseries in Strathclyde, Kelly
(1995) encountered many instances of an alarming nature where the
parents were simply not able to cope with the responsibilities of caring for
their own children. The worst such cases involved horrific abuse, with
children being physically and sexually assaulted or, even worse, being
thrown out of windows! Such situations present the early years professional with an enormous challenge, one that, if taken seriously, will lead
to a re-definition of what it means to be a professional.

But not all vulnerabilities are quite so dramatic. If a family experiences
economic hardship or is a lone-parent family, or a large family, or a
family with a special need or an ethnic minority family or indeed, any
combination of these (Tennant, 1995), then stress can impinge on the
relationships between parents and children. Support in such circumstances is increasingly important. But if that support is not forthcoming
from traditional sources — family, friends and neighbours — it is left to
the state to act.

3.3 Expanding provision

We want to ensure that a range of good quality childcare is available
in every community which allows parents to choose childcare which
meets their needs. (The Scottish Office, 1998a, p 19)

In the 1999 White Paper, the Government made a commitment to
providing a quality education place for every 4-year old immediately and
for every 3-year old by 2002, should the parents wish it. In addition, new
funds were allocated from the Lottery Revenues to expand out-of-school
care and provision for under-threes.

It was proposed that expansion of places be achieved through the mixed-economy model of provision, i.e. that a means be found to facilitate access to those families who wish it to flexible provision in the independent and voluntary sectors as well as to increase the number of places in the public sector. A partnership arrangement — called *local childcare partnerships* — was therefore initiated, involving all three types of provider (see Section 3.5).

This partnership or plural approach to expansion depended on services being responsive to three factors: parental views, personal circumstances and children's preferences. Such recognition of the need for flexible services was far removed from the situation in previous times, where the take-it-or-leave-it provision, if indeed it was available, predominated. But for parents to make informed choices, adequate information regarding the availability of services was essential. The Childcare Strategy document recognised this need and proposed to provide:

- Advice on what to look for in a childcare service
- Help in deciding upon the most suitable arrangement for their children, particularly for children with special needs
- Up-to-date details on what childcare places are available in the area where they live or work

(The Scottish Office, 1998a, p 21)

The need for information both for employers and new childcare providers was also noted. It was deemed to be the task of the proposed new childcare partnership to develop the required range of information to the relevant stakeholders.

3.4 The costs of childcare

Traditionally, in the UK, early childhood services in the public sector have been free to those families who were given access. However, places in that sector have until now been limited. In 1995/6 only 38% of 4-year olds attended a state-funded nursery school or class. Places in the independent sector are expensive and have only been accessible to those parents with sufficient disposable income. Fees per child per week vary between £100 and £150, which is well outwith the financial reach of many families. On the other hand, places in the voluntary sector provision — playgroups, mother/toddler groups — have been relatively inexpensive. However, such provision is largely 'sessional' i.e. a place for a few hours per day, two or three times per week. In addition, it has been the well-defended practice of the voluntary sector to involve parents — usually mothers — in the delivery of such services. For many families, however, such provision was quite inadequate for their needs, particularly if the parents were employed. Thus, prior to 2000, different families paid widely different amounts, depending on the type of care and education they wished for their children.

In the Childcare Strategy, the Government gave the undertaking to provide free part-time places (i.e. 5 half days per week) for every 4-year old in Scotland subject to parental wishes, and for every 3-year old from 2002. To ensure parity with the public sector, this meant that public funds had to be channelled to families who wished to access the provision in the independent and voluntary sectors. The mechanism introduced to achieve this was the childcare tax credit as part of the Working Families Tax Credit targeted at low and middle income families. Figure 3.1 provides details of the system as specified in the Childcare Strategy.

Figure 3.1: The Childcare Strategy for Scotland: the childcare tax credit arrangements

---

The childcare tax credit

Any lone parent working 16 hours a week or more, and paying for childcare, will be eligible for the childcare tax credit. Couples will also be eligible where both partners are working for 16 hours or more a week.

The childcare tax credit will:

- Cover up to 70 per cent of eligible costs of approved childcare, up to a maximum of £70 a week for families with one child and £105 for families with two or more children. Registered care, childcare on school premises (e.g. out of school clubs) and certain other places exempt from registration are all eligible. These limits have been chosen to ensure that the credit makes a reasonable contribution to a family's childcare costs, while encouraging families to make the most cost-effective use of childcare;
- Be structured so that the lowest earning families will get help and the poorest families will benefit in full.
- Give a couple with two children and income below £330 per week (£17,000 per year) the full 70 per cent of their eligible childcare costs;
- Reach higher up the income distribution than Family Credit. For example, a couple with two young children who earn £23,400 a year might receive as much as £45 a week.

Source: The Scottish Office, 1998a, p 17

The prime purpose of the arrangements as outlined in Figure 3.1 was to ensure that childcare became more affordable for families who needed it. It was also proposed in the Childcare Strategy Paper to provide financial help with childcare costs to students (both full-time and part-time) and for parents engaged in training courses.

3.5 Implementation of the Strategy

Crucial to the delivery of the Strategy was the willingness of all those involved in providing care and education services to families with young children to enter into partnership arrangements.

> Central and local government, other statutory agencies, employers, parents and private, public and voluntary sector childcare providers, among others, have a vital role to play. (The Scottish Office, 1998a, p 25)

At the centre of this partnership policy was the establishment of *local childcare partnerships* in every local authority area (Scottish Executive, 1999c). Such partnerships were charged with the implementation of the expansion of the system outlined in the Childcare Strategy, i.e. free places for 3- and 4-year old children in a mixed-economy model, subject to parental wishes. Initially, under leadership from respective local authority staff, they were expected to conduct an audit of local availability of places provided by each of the main providers, that is, the local authority, the private and the voluntary sectors, and to match this against the extent of demand for more or longer places. Following this, plans had to be drawn up to harmonise availability and demand. Local childcare partnerships were also given a role in advising the New Opportunities Fund in relation to application for support from its out-of-school childcare programme.

At national level, the Strategy Paper proposed the establishment of a Scottish Childcare Board *to advise Ministers on objectives and priorities for Scotland as a whole and in so doing so draw out particular issues for different areas*. But delivering the Strategy also requires investment of very considerable resources if it is to succeed. The Scottish Executive has indicated that it is willing to provide such resources. The next chapter explores the fundamental reasons why the Executive has taken a quantum leap forward by expanding early childhood education and care in Scotland.

CHAPTER 4

WHY EARLY CHILDHOOD EDUCATION?

4.1 Introduction

The importance of early childhood education was drawn to national attention by the report of Sir Christopher Ball — *Start right, the importance of early learning*, published by the Royal Society of Arts):

> This report presents a challenge to the nation — to parents, educators, employers, parliament — indeed to our society as a whole. It demonstrates the importance of early learning as a preparation for effective education to promote social welfare and social order, and to develop a world class workforce. (Ball, 1994, p 6)

The key benefit of early childhood education was seen by Ball in terms of enhancing children's learning, in order to promote a better society in the longer term. The evidence for this is undoubtedly strong (Sylva and Wiltshire, 1994) but it would be somewhat shortsighted just to regard the advantages of early childhood education solely in terms of the direct benefits to children. This is not to question the priority of promoting children's development and learning. This is paramount. However, there are other advantages that not only indirectly benefit children further but contribute to the quality of family life and the prosperity of society as a whole.

First, there is the benefit to the parenting process. Being a parent in modern times is a demanding and challenging, though rewarding, role — particularly for mothers. If there is no support available, which is often the case in rural areas, the stress of parental responsibility can be crippling. Young children are demanding beings. Their inquisitiveness, their search for understanding, their sociability, their disregard of danger, their innocence and their unending questioning can exert a considerable price on the carers' patience, understanding and well-being, particularly if it is undertaken without support and even more so if the child has a special need. Having access to good-quality, affordable services helps to provide this support mainly, though not exclusively, to mothers. Having 'space' to be oneself without the constant demands of child-rearing responsibilities is a god-send to most, and a life-line to some. But sending one's children to a local nursery or playgroup does not signal the abdication of parental responsibilities. The education and care of young children needs to be an effective partnership between the two, where communication, dialogue and flexibility are cornerstones. Parents still need to maintain consistent approaches to their children, not least the moral dimension to what it means to be human, particularly in terms of right and wrong, a point recognised by White (1999) in her argument that the fostering of civic virtues can and should begin in early childhood.

Secondly, there is a potential economic benefit to the family, and hence to wider society, of early childhood education. The modern pluralist family requires to be economically viable. This often means that the parent, or both parents, will be in paid employment. In the case of a single-parent family which, according to Tisdall and Donaghy (1995), comprise some 16% of all families in Scotland, the demands of work and child-rearing are too often in stark contrast, even if early childhood education and care is available. Nevertheless, having appropriate and flexible childcare available for working parents is a necessity of modern life. In turn, this can give the family more freedom and contribute to the family's quality of life.

Thirdly, there is the benefit to the wider society, both in the short and longer term. In the short term, if the parents' economic activity is facilitated by good childcare arrangements, this ensures more effective social inclusion and contributes to the tax revenues. In the longer term the research shows that there are less demands on the resources of society for someone with a good early childhood education. Results from the High/Scope Perry Pre-school study in the USA shows that:

...by the age of 27 the High/Scope 'pre-school graduate' had
* Higher monthly earnings
* Higher percentage of home ownership and of second car ownership
* A higher level of schooling completed
* A lower percentage receiving social services at some time in the past ten years
* Fewer arrests, including fewer arrested for crimes of drug-taking or dealing.

(Ball, 1994, p 17)

It is almost beyond belief that early childhood education can be so influential. But, as both Watt (1994) and Osborn (1994) point out, expecting such dramatic improvements in British society as a consequence of universal early childhood education would be dangerous. The High/Scope projects were not typical early years contexts.

Fourthly, there is evidence that early childhood education can help to raise attainment in the formal school sector. Shorrocks (1993) undertook a systematic follow-up study of childrne at the age of seven, half of whom had pre-school experience, in which she controlled for socio-economic background. Her study showed:

- there were significant differences in favour of those with nursery experience in both English and Mathematics, but not for Science
- children with pre-school experience scored significantly higher in reading and writing
- in Mathematics, the picture was less clear: many of the Attainment Targets showed similar significant differences, but interestingly not those concerned with number work
- in Science, there were significant differences in many of the Attainment Targets, but not in the one concerned with the processes of scientific thinking

(Shorrocks, 1993, p 4)

4.2 Learning and Development in Early Childhood

Few would challenge the notion that the primary purpose of early childhood education is to promote children's development and learning. Both 'development' and 'learning' are key features of young children as they negotiate their way through the myriad of experience they encounter. The two concepts are by no means identical but are inextricably linked: each reinforces the other.

Whatever experiences children encounter, learning is taking place. Children learn from day-to-day contexts — the home, the nursery, the street, even the supermarket. 'What' children learn, however, is problematic. Some learning is clearly more beneficial than other forms of learning. Nevertheless, most learning tends to be positive in the sense that it helps children to understand their world better, it provides them with knowledge and know-how and helps them become more aware, not only of themselves but also of others and the environment in which they live. But learning can also be negative. Some children easily acquire facets of anti-social behaviour, particularly if treated inappropriately, for whatever reason, by parents and other children. In such situations, early childhood education and care can be of critical importance (Wilkinson, 1995).

Promoting positive learning is the task of good parents and effective early years professionals working in partnership. In their book *Promoting children's learning from birth to five*, Anning and Edwards (1999) argue for a theory of children's learning based on socio-cultural psychology:

> Socio-cultural psychology tells us that learning is a process of being able to participate increasingly effectively in the world in which we find ourselves. (Anning and Edwards, 1999, p 61)

Key to such a theory is the role of experience. So much depends on how children see, interpret and respond to the learning opportunities available to them, irrespective of whether these opportunities are self-directed, as in play, or whether they are mediated by adults, as in listening to stories. Learning occurs in contexts which are mediated by the culture in which children live. Active participation on the part of children is therefore essential, and that requires positive interaction with people and with tasks. Encouragement of such engagement is a central role for adults, where play experience is crucial. Children's participation is not achieved through passive observation or by instruction: it requires the direct engagement in children's mental and physical activities.

Although the emphasis over the past few years has been on what children learn in the form of national curriculum guidelines, the 'how' issue is just as important. Helping children to learn in a meaningful way requires adults, as Anning and Edwards suggest, to engage in *careful observation as the precursor to leading children through guided participation, towards new learning.*

4.3 Support for the family

As indicated in Chapter 1, the 'family' in modern times is vastly different from what it was 50 or even 20 years ago. The family as a norm no longer exists. In contemporary times children are brought up in very diverse family environments — foster families, lone-parent families, gay families, co-habiting families and two-parent families (Muncie, et al. 1995). Many of these diverse families are not without their controversies. For example, in the contemporary debate about appropriate and inappropriate family arrangements, a number of religious leaders have taken a stance against lesbian families on moral grounds as undermining the 'natural' arrangement whereby a family consists of a mother and a father in a marriage relationship with at least one child, preferably more.

A significant body of research now exists to support the view that *children raised in lesbian mother families become well adjusted adults* (Golombok, 2002) The most recent study by Golombok et al. (2002) is a longitudinal investigation based on a sample of 14,000 mothers and their children in Bristol, beginning in pregnancy. The study found that children raised in lesbian families did not show a higher incidence of psychological disorder, or of difficulties in peer relationships than did children from heterosexual homes. Its conclusions support the view that in the 21st century a lesbian sexual orientation should no longer be considered to be a reason to deny a mother the custody of her children.

The defence of diversity (or pluralism) in family life is often conducted on the quality of the relationships inside the family. What is important is that children feel safe and secure, they are loved, they are well cared for and they are given opportunities to learn and develop in a positive, sensitive and stable environment. Many would claim that the formal relationship in structural terms between the adults, or whether there is only one parent, is irrelevant, providing that the child's interests are taken seriously. But this is not a universal position. Many commentators still support the notion of the traditional family. However, the growth of the pluralistic family presents the early years professionals with an immense challenge, one in which the professional's own personal values are brought into sharp focus. It will not be easy for many nursery nurses/nursery teachers to work in partnership with a family if the family composition is ideologically at odds with their own values.

All too often, however, the family is not the haven of warmth, security and solidarity. Acute domestic tensions — sometimes domestic violence — can work against children's well-being. In such situations the support provided by early childhood services is a lifeline and child protection becomes a modern-day necessity. Nursery nurses, nursery teachers, playleaders and others have constantly to be vigilant for family-generated transgressions against children, for example, physical abuse. It is in such situations that diligent observation, backed up with rapid inter-agency support, is vital. This support requires the integration of services not too dissimilar from that evident in community nurseries (Wilkinson, 1995) and now embedded in the concept of the new community school (The Scottish Office, 1998b). But finding an appropriate balance between support, child protection and surveillance in the context of inter-professional collaboration is not unproblematic.

In order for early years professionals to work in partnership with families in the education and care of children, awareness of social policies in relation to the family is increasingly important. Profound processes of change in everyday life are now occurring which cannot be ignored. In terms of lone parents in Scotland, Tisdall and Donaghy (1995) found that:

- 16% of all Scottish households with children are headed by lone parents
- 9 out of 10 lone parents are women
- 13 out of 19 lone parent households are headed by mothers who have been married
- The majority of lone mothers are classified as 'economically inactive'. A Scottish Enterprise survey of the potential female workforce found that over half were unable to work due to family responsibility and lack of corresponding services and support.

(Tisdall and Donaghy, 1995, p 9)

According to European statistics compiled by Roll (1992), Scotland is only second to Denmark in the percentage of households with children headed by a lone parent.

In terms of gender differences in economic activity the trends for men and women in Scotland are diametrically opposed. Between 1981 and 1991 economically inactive males between the ages of 16 and 59 rose by 5% whilst the percentage of economically inactive women of the same age range fell by the same amount. (Tisdall & Donaghy, 1995). Data from the Central Statistical Office (1995) show that nearly 50% of all women with the youngest child aged 0–5 years are now in paid employment, though with two-thirds in part-time occupations. For some families, with both parents working, there has been an improvement in their economic circumstances. For many, however, there has been deterioration. Tennant (1995) found that the percentage of children living in poverty (defined as household income below 50% of the national average) rose from 10% in 1979 to 32% in 1992. In the 1990's therefore, 1 in 3 children were brought up in poverty and the ratio is still rising in the new millennium. Unfortunately, families in poverty tend to be concentrated in inner city areas or peripheral housing schemes attached to the major cities. Recent data, for instance, based on the former Scottish office Revised Area Deprivation Index (The Scottish Office, 1998c), have shown that the depth of poverty in such cities as Glasgow is nearly double the national average (Wilkinson, Baron and Schad, 2002). Even within Glasgow the situation in which children are living varies enormously. For example, in Easterhouse the proportion of families on income support is five times the national average (Wilkinson, Baron and Schad, 2002). Most children in Easterhouse live in conditions of *unrelenting material deprivation*. Such stark reality cannot be ignored by governments.

As stated in Chapter 2, Third Way politics strongly influence contemporary social policy on the family:

> The family is a basic institution of civil society. Family policy is a key test for the new politics: is there a politics of the family beyond neo-liberalism and old-style social democracy? (Giddens, 1998, p 89)

Central features of such a family policy are: the acceptance of diversity, equality between the sexes, and the supporting role of the state.

On the former, given the diverse nature of contemporary pluralistic families, the avoidance of discrimination is crucial. The policy requires that there is a range of childcare services to choose from so that families are not stigmatised. Furthermore, the early years professional must be ready to respond to family issues as they arise, irrespective of whether the family is the traditional two-parent family or whether, for example, the parents are lesbian.

On the sexual equality issue, debate is focused on the role of fathers in the caring process (Henwood, 1987), particularly if there has been a divorce between the parents. Finding meaningful ways of supporting all fathers to maintain supportive contact with their children is not easy. But it would be wrong to think that fathers who lose contact with their children are all 'bad men'. As Giddens puts it:

> The large majority of men don't feel relief at having shed their responsibilities for their children. Most attempt to sustain their relationships with them, even in the face of great difficulties. Many who lose contact do so because of the emotional traumas involved, or the active hostility of the ex-partner, rather than a desire to follow an errant lifestyle. (Giddens, 1998, p 96)

The challenge for the early years professional on this issue is difficult.

Many would argue that *fathers should have greater parenting rights than at present, but they should be provided, where necessary, with the means to discharge their responsibilities* (Giddens, 1998). Supporting fathers in accepting their responsibilities is a new challenge for early years professionals, a challenge that all professionals might not willingly accept. But democratic families imply shared responsibility for childcare, especially greater sharing between the sexes and among parents and family members who are not necessarily the biological parent. Third Way policies are targeted at promoting greater parental responsibility both to children and the wider society:

> Strong family ties can be an effective source of civic cohesion only if they look outwards as well as inwards — this is what I mean by the socially integrated family. (Giddens, 1998, p 98)

Thirdly, on the role of the state in family affairs, the Third Way advocates a strong, supportive involvement of government. On the one hand it seeks democratisation of the family where individual choice and social solidarity sit together, albeit at times rather uncomfortably. According to Giddens:

> Democratization in the context of the family implies equality, mutual respect, autonomy, decision-making through communication and freedom from violence. (Giddens, 1998, p 93)

In addition, it seeks to support those families with financial hardship. The Working Families Tax Credit is means-tested in favour of those families with low and middle incomes to facilitate access to quality childcare provision (see Chapter 4)

It is therefore seen by many as the role of the state to support families by providing access to high-quality services, flexible enough to meet the diverse needs of every individual family unit.

The New Labour Government has put in place a range of policies to support the family, the most robust of which is the Working Families Tax Credit. Such financial support to families with children under the age of 16 supports families to access early years services and out-of-school services if not accessible in the public sector (See Chapter 4). Such a policy is a clear statement to the effect that the state has a responsibility to support families in bringing up children. It also implies that the bringing up of children is a joint responsibility between the state and the family. The family is no longer entirely the private province of parents, nor are children exclusively 'owned' by their parents. What happens behind 'closed-doors' has now been brought within the domain of the state, for better or for worse (see Chapter 6). It is now opportune for ordinary citizens to exercise a degree of civic responsibility and point out to parents who inflict painful physical and psychological abuse on their children in public places that this behaviour is no longer tolerable.

4.4 Working parents

The third benefit of early childhood services is the potential freedom which services bring to economic activity in the family. If the parents (or parent) are confident and can have peace of mind that their child is being well cared for in a safe, stimulating and challenging environment, the parents (most often the mother) can participate in work, whether through economic necessity, psychological support or both. Over the past 25 years more and more mothers have entered the labour market, with the consequent demand for more flexible childcare. Well over half of women with children under 5 now work. The issue of 'working parents' is inextricably bound up with influential pressure groups such as the women's movement. Many women with children no longer see themselves solely as mothers but as inter-dependent adults on equal terms with men. More opportunities and choices are now available to women than ever before. This fundamental shift in opportunity has now penetrated most developed countries though it is still biased against the lower socio-economic groups. The trend for more social inclusion for women can also be seen in the attainment levels in schools. Over the past 25 years girls have gradually been achieving higher results in school; and the differentiation is not limited to formal school. At the age of 3 and 4 years gender differences have also emerged (Wilkinson et al., 2001) which have major significance for the future of our society. (See Chapter 7).

But is this trend for more working parents good for children? Some would argue that the 'demand' on mothers to work places them in a very invidious position. At times children are neglected. In such situations early childhood education and care have a vital role to play. In countries where it is the cultural norm for parents to work (for example, Denmark) the state provides extensive early childhood services to suit the needs of the parents. There is no evidence to suggest that children are disadvantaged in such circumstances.

Not until fairly recently has it become widespread in the UK for mothers with young children to work way from the family home. This has been particularly pronounced where the children are under 3 years of age. In sustaining this attitude, the work of Bowlby (1952) on the psychological consequences for children of maternal deprivation has been tantalisingly influential.

The debate about whether working mothers can have a detrimental effect on their child's health still remains unresolved. The work of Belsky (2001) supports the view that, if a child is placed in childcare outside the home for more than 20 hours per week when the child is under one year of age, there are some detectable negative effects (see Chapter 6).

4.5 Raising standards

The fourth potential benefit of early childhood education and care is, in a sense, more political. Experience of early childhood education seems to give children a distinct advantage when they encounter formal education in the school system. The evidence from the US on this issue is impressive (Berruta-Clement et al., 1984). Although such studies cannot prove that all pre-school education will bring lasting benefits, they demonstrate that early childhood education *can change the course of children's lives, especially those from disadvantaged backgrounds* (Sylva and Wiltshire, 1994). Given such a finding, the temptation of policy-makers has been to encourage early childhood education settings to over-formalise young children's education. This has been particularly pronounced in the Reception classes for 4-year olds in England.

Since 1979 both Conservative and Labour governments have been concerned to find ways of raising standards in the school system. In Scotland, a Task Force reported to the then Secretary of State *on strategies to improve performance in primary and secondary schools* (SOEID, 1996). The concept of *Early Intervention* was enshrined in the report:

> The Task Force gives highest priority to a comprehensive strategy for strengthening the delivery of education in the early years of schooling, and to programmes of planned intervention for pupils in nursery and P1 to P3. (Scottish Education & Industry Department, 1996, p 1)

Not surprisingly, however, given that the Task Force was established by a Conservative government, it did not recommend expansion of pre-school education resourced from public funds.

Similarly, the Labour Government elected in 1997 put forward radical proposals to Parliament in 1999, the core of which was aimed at raising attainment:

> Education is central to the Government's fundamental objective of promoting social inclusion. While educational attainment by itself cannot right all wrongs associated with poverty and deprivation, it can make a major difference. (The Scottish Office, 1999c, p 3)

Fortunately, in Scotland, there has been little such pressure either from parents or policy-makers. In its White Paper on Education in 1999 — *Targeting Excellence — Modernising Scotland's Schools* — the Labour Government reinforced the importance of good-quality, pre-school education:

> The Government recognises the importance of pre-school education and wants to see all children whose parents wish it benefit from pre-school education from the term after their third birthday. (The Scottish Office, 1999c, p 7)

It is early days to ascertain whether such universal provision will make a major contribution to the promotion of a better society. But many are very hopeful.

CHAPTER 5

EARLY IMPACT OF THE NEW CHILDCARE STRATEGY

5.1 Introduction

Implementation of the Childcare Strategy for Scotland is now the responsibility of the Scottish Executive. In Chapter 3, the three main strands of the Childcare Strategy were outlined. These were:

- to expand provision
- to make childcare more affordable and available
- to raise the quality of care

Each year, in September, the Scottish Executive publishes statistics on the number of children in pre-school education and daycare centres. These statistics enable us to track how well the Executive is delivering the first strand of its strategy to expand provision. Tracking progress on the other two strands, however, is more problematic. Developments in quality enhancement are now the responsibility of the new Scottish Commission on the Regulation of Care, whilst information on the financial commitment of the Executive to Working Families Tax Credit is within the realm of the Finance Minister and the Public Spending Review conducted each year.

5.2 Expanding places

Statistics on the expansion of the early childhood education system in Scotland (see website — html//www.scotland.gov.uk/stats/bulletins) show that at the beginning of 2002, 96% of all 4-year olds and 85% of all 3-year olds were accessing early childhood care and education services, such services being available in an estimated 4,117 locations the length and breadth of Scotland (Scottish Executive, 2002a). Although these data may be subject to exaggeration due to 'double-counting' (that is, children attending multiple locations per week) by any standard they represent a quantum leap forward from 1996/7, which was the last year in office of the then Conservative Government.

The statistics also show that nearly 75% of children attending pre-school provision were doing so in public sector services, with the remainder in the private and voluntary sectors (see Table 5.1). Table 5.2

provides a breakdown of the ages of children attending services in the three sectors.

Table 5.1: Number of children receiving pre-school education by academic year, mode of attendance and management type of centre: January 2002[1]

Centre Type	Number of half days attended per week[2]	All Years	Ante pre-school Year[3]	Pre-school year (normal age)[4]	Pre-school year (deferred entry)[5]
All types	**Total**	**98,769**	**41,186**	**54,068**	**3,515**
	10	13,379	4,520	8,122	737
	6 to 9	4,940	2,122	2,662	156
	5	67,254	25,451	39,422	2,381
	1 to 4	13,196	9,093	3,862	241
Local Authority	**Total**	**72,566**	**26,604**	**43,063**	**2,899**
	10	9,948	3,082	6,247	619
	6 to 9	2,264	818	1,350	96
	5	55,344	19,868	33,429	2,047
	1 to 4	5,010	2,836	2,037	137
Partnership	**Total**	**26,203**	**14,582**	**11,005**	**616**
	10	3,431	1,438	1,875	118
	6 to 9	2,676	1,304	1,312	60
	5	11,910	5,583	5,993	334
	1 to 4	8,186	6,257	1,825	104

Notes:
1 Includes all children receiving pre-school education in centres run by a local authority or commissioned by a local authority to provide pre-school education.
2 The number of sessions attended as shown here is the total number of sessions attended by a child regardless of the source of funding for those sessions.
3 Ante pre-school year consists of children born between 1st March 1998 and 28th February 1999.
4 Pre-school year consists of children born between 1st March 1997 and 28th February 1998.
5 Pre-school year children for whom entry is deferred were born before 1st March 1997.

Source: Statistical Bulletin, Scottish Executive (2002a)

Early Childhood Education

Table 5.2: Number of children attending pre-school education or daycare centres by age of child and main type of facility: January 2002

| | Main type of facility | | | | | | |
Age of child	Nursery	Playgroup	Playscheme	Out of school Care Club	Creche	Family Centre	Total
Under 1 year old	2,304	277	5	11	546	338	3,481
1 year old	5,094	783	71	48	955	803	7,754
2 years old	9,351	6,000	128	121	2,761	2,073	20,434
3 years old	33,501	12,213	222	421	2,226	2,061	50,644
4 years old	50,110	4,928	193	440	2,947	1,712	60,330
5 years old	11,047	372	475	2,975	1,656	687	17,212
6 years old	1,094	41	536	3,469	750	504	6,394
7 years old	439	20	577	3,554	713	413	5,716
8 years old and over	1,265	96	1,651	11,211	431	1,789	16,443
Total number of children	114,205	24,730	3,858	22,250	12,985	10,380	118,408

Source: Statistical Bulletin 00192-00, Scottish Executive (2002a)

Examining the distribution between the three types of service provider — the public, the private and the voluntary sectors — the data in Figure 5.2 clearly show that the vast majority of 3-year olds attended playgroups in the voluntary sector whereas the majority of 4-year olds were in nursery, either in the public or private sectors. This seems to suggest that many parents are regarding different childhood education and care services as sequential by first sending their child to playgroup then subsequently to nursery school/class. This being the case, questions need to be raised about the impact on children's development and learning from moving location at least three times over the span of two or three years — home, playgroup, nursery, then primary school.

The statistics also indicate that the vast majority (86.5%) of children attended a pre-school centre on a part-time basis. However, the distribution of part-time and full-time attendance varied between the different types of provision and by age. Drawing on the data in Table 5.1, percentages have been calculated to illustrate this difference of attendance patterns and is provided in Table 5.3.

Table 5.3: Attendance patterns (%) of 3- and 4-year old children in publicly supported early years provision in Scotland

		Ante- pre-school year (i.e. 3-year olds	Pre-school year (i.e. 4-year olds)
Public Sector	*Part-time*	88.4	85.5
	Full-time	11.6	14.5
Private/voluntary Sector in partner-	*Part-time*	90.1	83.0
ship with an LA	*Full-time*	9.9	17.0

It can be seen from Table 5.3 that, in relative terms, there is a slight tendency for parents who can get access to full-time early years provision for 4-year olds do so in the partnership private sector (there being very little full-time provision in the voluntary sector) whereas for 3-year olds there is a preference for the public sector. However, in absolute terms, twice as many 3-year olds and three times as many 4-year olds attend public sector provision on a full-time basis compared to the private sector.

Given that in many families parents work, the provision of childcare services in Scotland is still inadequate to facilitate full-time work by parents, should they wish to do so. From research undertaken by Stephen, Brown, Cope and Waterhouse into the experiences of 3- and 4-year old children in all-day provision it was concluded that:

The study focused exclusively on what constitutes *good all-day provision* and acknowledged that, despite rapid expansion in part-time provision, this did not meet the increasing needs of working parents. (Stephen et al., 2001, p i)

In addition, it was found that:

The observations of children and the conversations with them suggested that their experience of all-day provision was predominantly satisfactory, regardless of the type of provision they experienced. (Stephen et al., 2001, p 97)

More needs to be done therefore to transform existing services — particularly nursery schools and classes — to provide more full-time, all-day, all-year places on a flexible basis. In their book, *Transforming Nursery Education*, Moss and Penn (1996) chart the way forward for this transformation. Clearly there is still a long way to go in Scotland.

5.3 Improving the quality of provision

There are three sources of information to allow judgements to be made on the extent to which quality in early childhood education and care is improving. These are:

- reports from HM Inspectorate of Education
- reports from local authorities
- individual studies

5.31

In *Standards and Quality in Scottish Pre-school Education — 1997–2001* (HMIE, 2002), the outcome of inspections across the three sectors — local authority, independent and voluntary — over a four-year period is reported, though the inspections in the independent and voluntary sectors are limited to those centres that were working in partnership with a local authority. From 1995 to August 2000, the evaluations made by HMIE were based on the document *Using Performance Indicators in Nursery schools/class/and pre-five unit* published in 1995. From August 2000 the basis of the HMIE evaluations changed to *The Child at the Centre* (Scottish Executive, 2000a). The key findings were:

- A high proportion of nursery schools and classes achieved high or very high standards in most aspects inspected
- In almost all centres there were good relationships with parents and a strong, supportive ethos
- Almost all nursery schools and classes and most private and voluntary centres offered broad and well-balanced programmes, and children engaged well in their activities

- Almost all centres in all sectors were providing good or very good programmes to support children's emotional, personal and social development
- In almost all nursery schools and classes, and most private and voluntary centres, staff interacted well with the children to encourage and support their learning and development
- Staff teamwork was good or very good in all but a very few centres
                                                    (HMI of Education, 2002, p 4)

The findings show that a large proportion of children are experiencing a high quality of pre-school education in Scotland though there is still scope for considerable improvement in private and voluntary services, particularly in the application of systematic planning (see Figure 5.4).

Figure 5.4: Scottish pre-school centres considered by HMIE to be of good or very good quality (%)

	Local authority/ Independent schools	Voluntary Sector	Independent Sector
Emotional, Personal and Social Development	99	91	94
Communication and Language	94	72	76
Knowledge and Under-Standing of the World	94	71	77
Expressive & Aesthetic Development	92	70	71
Physical Development & Movement	88	75	75
Scope and balance	95	74	77
Planning	73	46	49

Source: HMIE Report on Standards & Quality in Scottish Pre-school Education (2002)

Enhancing quality, however, is a dynamic process. There is a continual scope for improvement even if quality ratings are high. It was not surprising therefore that HMIE identified the need for further improvements. These included:

- more effective links with other agencies
- more streamlined planning
- better use of assessment information

- curricular improvements in the independent and voluntary sectors
- more continuing professional development
- more rigorous self-evaluation

The inspectorate concluded that:

> Overall, the quality of educational provision across the centres inspected was high, and often very high. There were examples of high quality provision across all sectors of pre-school education.

> Provision in voluntary and private pre-school has shown improvements in a number of important areas over the last four years. (HMI of Education, 2002, p 4)

The improvements sought by HMIE are matters that contribute to the process of quality enhancement for all early years settings not just those deemed to be adequate. A crucial improvement is the recognition that better use needs to be made of assessment information.

However, assessment of children's educational achievements in early childhood education has recently become a controversial issue, not least because of the dual purpose of such assessments. On the one hand, systematic assessments are desirable in order to:

> provide information on children's educational attainment and help teachers plan effectively to meet children's individual learning needs (the pedagogic imperative). (Wilkinson et al., 2001a, p 33)

Whilst, on the other hand, they are increasingly regarded as indications of the effectiveness of early years settings:

> to assess children's attainment using one or more numerical outcomes which can be used in later value-added analysis of children's progress (the managerial imperative). (Wilkinson et al., 2001a, p 33)

In recent times, assessment of children in the early years has been referred to as baseline assessment. Its origins can be traced back to the concerns of the last Conservative government in its drive to raise educational standards in the formal school system. The 1997 Labour Government, and more recently the Scottish Executive, have endorsed such policies.

At the end of the 1990's a research and development (R & D) initiative undertaken in Scotland explored the feasibility of introducing a national baseline assessment scheme. One of the tensions identified by the R & D team was between adopting a quasi-psychometric approach to assessment (that is, 'testing') as opposed to an approach based on the judgement of professional early years staff. Schemes that adopted the testing approach (for example, the PIPS scheme — see Tymms, 1996) claimed greater reliability and consistency, whereas advocates of the approach based on professional judgement (that is, formative assessment) claimed greater educational validity (Black and Wiliam, 1998).

The R & D team in Scotland, consisting of widely experienced early years professionals and experienced researchers, took the view that a national baseline assessment scheme based on formative assessment was more likely to have a positive effect on children's learning than a scheme based on tests. The scheme that was devised by the R & D team after an extensive review of schemes elsewhere (see Wilkinson and Napuk, 1997) involved three stages:

Stage 1: formative assessment of children in their pre-school year by teachers and nursery nurses, based on eight 'aspects of learning'. Common to both the Curriculum Framework 3–5 and the Curriculum Guidelines 5–14, each child being rated on a 1–4 scale on each aspect of learning.

Stage 2: automatic transfer of the assessment information to the appropriate primary school as a basis for planning P1 activities.

Stage 3: a second formative assessment of children at the end of their first year in P1, together with value-added information, as a basis for planning and resourcing activities in P2 and beyond.

An evaluation of the pilot scheme was undertaken by the researchers in the R & D team (Wilkinson, Johnson, Watt, Napuk and Normand, 2001b). Although some teachers and pre-school staff found the task demanding, most welcomed the approach. As a consequence of the findings from the evaluation, certain modifications were made to the original scheme and the title of the scheme changed from baseline assessment to the Transition Record, in recognition of the increasing variation in the age at which children start their early years experience. In addition, staff development material to support the use of the Transition Record has now been made available.

It is now regarded as good practice in early childhood education that assessment information such as that generated in the Transition Record can play a vital role in ensuring that all children engage with the learning process as effectively as possible.

5.32
Turning to the data available from local authorities, one of the most comprehensive reports on both public and partnership nurseries was published by Renfrewshire Council in 2001 in Council Nurseries (Renfrewshire Council, 2001a and b). Based on the Council's own reviews, Figure 5.5 shows a comparison between public and partnership nurseries (both independent and voluntary) between 1997 and 2000 on a range of indicators.

Figure 5.5: Comparison of quality of early childhood education — a case in a Scottish local authority area

	Public Sector	Private & Voluntary Sector in Partnership
Accommodation/Resources	88	88
Learning & development	95	91
Effectiveness	96	75
Management & Quality Assurance	90	59
Curriculum areas*		
– emotional, personal & social development	3.5	3.5
– communication/language	3.6	3.2
– knowledge of understanding	3.1	3.3
– physical development/ movement	3.5	3.1
– expressive & aesthetic development	3.3	3.3

* on a scale 1–4 with 4 being the highest

As with the HMIE findings, nurseries in partnership with the local authority in Renfrewshire are clearly comparable with nurseries in the public sector with the exception of their management and quality assurance procedures. Clearly not all nurseries in the private and voluntary sectors are using rigorous quality assurance schemes, nor keeping apace with current developments in management procedures.

5.33
A third source of information about quality in early childhood education and care is to be found in individual research projects, though as yet there is no systematic study conducted in Scotland on the impact on quality of the implementation of the Childcare Strategy.

Based on the Early Childhood Environment Rating Scale (ECERS) (Harms & Clifford, 1980) Stephen and Wilkinson undertook comparisons between different types of provision in the public sector as part of their work on the effectiveness of Strathclyde Region's new community nurseries. Analysing ratings undertaken by experts using the seven ECERS scales, they compared two nursery schools with two community nurseries. Not only did they demonstrate that extended day provision in the new community nurseries can achieve the same level of quality as highly reputable nursery schools, they also showed that over a period of time quality in the community nurseries improved as a direct consequence of feedback of information from ECERS (Stephen & Wilkinson, 1995).

However, the most extensive and exhaustive of such individual projects is that being undertaken by the Effective Provision of Pre-school Education (EPPI) Project based at the London Institute of Education. This is a five-year longitudinal study which began in 1997. Amongst other matters, the study aimed to compare and contrast the developmental progress of 3000+ children selected from a wide range of social and cultural backgrounds in six local authorities in England which have differing pre-school experiences. Using ECERS and its English Extension (ECERS-E) (Harms, Clifford and Cryer, 1998), comparisons were made between the different types of provider — public, private and voluntary. On the vast majority of indicators, nursery schools and classes were rated highest whilst playgroups in the voluntary sector were rated lowest, a finding not consistent with quality of provision in Scotland for those services in partnership with a local authority.

> This study shows clearly that well-resourced pre-school centres which had a history of 'education' (including a more substantial number of trained teachers, LEA in-service training, Ofsted 'Section 10' rather than 'pre-school Section 5' inspection) were providing the highest quality of care and education. The centres from the 'care' tradition, despite their more favourable ratios, were offering a different level of care and education. (Sylva et al., 2000, p 19)

Sylva et al. concluded in their interim report, however, that the standard of education and care in pre-school provision in England was adequate in the vast majority of settings.

A further indication of the quality of Scottish provision is to be found in the study of all-day provision undertaken by Stephen et al. in 2001.

> Three striking findings from this study were firstly the high levels of satisfaction with the provision expressed by parents, secondly, the indicators of positive responses from the children and, thirdly, the support for providers from the Curriculum Framework 3–5. (Stephen et al., 2001, p 101)

The task of raising quality in Scottish pre-school centres has now become the province of the new Scottish Commission on the Regulation of Care. The emergence of this Commission as a new 'player' in early years provision in Scotland will be addressed in the next chapter.

CHAPTER 6

PURSUIT OF QUALITY THROUGH REGULATIONS AND INTEGRATION

6.1 The emergence of the Scottish Care Commission

In its drive to enhance quality in early childhood services in Scotland, the Government believed *that early years education and childcare need to be subject to regulation backed by statute*. The Consultation Paper *Regulation of Early Education and Childcare* (The Scottish Office, 1999b) and the Government's White Paper *Aiming for Excellence* initiated the establishment of a new and important regulatory body, the Scottish Commission for the Regulation of Care (hitherto referred to as the 'Care Commission'). The aim of the Commission is *to ensure an improvement in the quality and services in Scotland, respecting the rights of people who use those services to dignity, choice and safety*.

In 2001 the Scottish Parliament created legislation in the form of the *Regulation of Care (Scotland) Act*, which formally set up the Care Commission. The establishment of the Commission represents a sea-change in the regulatory framework for early childhood education and care. Previously, the registration of daycare had been the legal responsibility of the local authorities under Part X of the Children Act 1989. This Act afforded local authorities a degree of flexibility in the registration of a person wishing to provide daycare either in the private or voluntary sector:

> Where a local authority register a person...they impose such reasonable requirements on him as they consider appropriate in his case. (Children Act, 1989, p 70)

In setting up the new Care Commission the regulatory responsibility of the local authorities was transferred to the Commission under the 2001 *Regulation of Care (Scotland)* Act. Part X of the 1989 Children Act, which had defined the previous regulatory framework, was repealed.

The 2001 Act is intended to ensure the attainment of unified national standards in all types of settings providing care for both children and adults outside the home. The general purpose of the standards is the protection and enhancement of safety, the welfare of all persons who use care services, and the promotion of diversity and choice in the provision of services. The case for protection by the state — particularly the protection of children — is largely based on the number of children being referred each year to social work departments for concerns about abuse. Over 7000 children are referred annually (Scottish Executive, 2002c) for suspected abuse. The Act identified 14 types of care services from adoption and fostering to independent health care, residential care for adults and the daycare of children including childminding. Within each type of care setting a National Care Standards Committee was given the task of developing the standards. In 2002 the care standards for early education and childcare up to the age of 16 were published (Scottish Executive, 2002b). For the purposes of the Act *daycare of children* was defined as:

> A service which consists of any form of care (whether or not provided to any extent in the form of an educational activity), supervised by a responsible person and not excepted from this definition by regulations, provided for children, on premises other than domestic premises, during the day. (Regulation of Care (Scotland) Act, 2001, p 5)

It was clear therefore that the Act and the new care standards would apply to daycare services in both the voluntary and private sectors with mandatory regulation by the Care Commission. The jurisdiction of the Commission in the public sector — nursery schools and classes — was less clear, it being recognised that local authority nursery schools and classes are subject to a different regulatory system under HMIE inspections.

However, the Scottish Executive's response to the 1999 consultation paper on regulation, where many consultees saw the creation of the Commission as an opportunity for better co-ordination or integration of registration and inspection regimes, stated that:

> We now intend that the Commission should also regulate local authority pre-school education provision. (Scottish Executive, 2000b, p 3)

The statement clearly indicated that the Scottish Executive wished to establish a common 'playing-field' for the three types of service provider — public, private and voluntary — as far as regulation was concerned. Inevitably, therefore, a tension between the Commission and HMI (the body hitherto responsible for monitoring standards in the public sector and partnership nurseries) would emerge. Discussions are currently under way between the Commission and HMIE to find a way forward for an integrated system of registration and inspection. A pilot scheme has recently been put in place.

6.2 The New Daycare Standards

The Care Commission has published 14 standards for early education and childcare up to the age of 16. They fall into three categories:

- Being welcomed and cared for (three standards)
- Confidence in the service (eight standards)
- Confidence in management (three standards)

Figure 6.1 shows the 14 standards in the three categories. Each of the standards has associated with it a number of criteria. In all, there are 55 criteria. The standards and their associated criteria are axiomatic for registration and inspection of all early years provision in Scotland.

> The standards will be taken into account by the Care Commission in making any decision about applications for registration (including varying or removing a condition that may have been imposed on the registration of the service). All providers must provide a statement of function and purpose when they are applying to register their service. On the basis of that statement, the Care Commission will determine which standards will apply to the service that the provider is offering. (Scottish Executive, 2002b, p 8)

Many of the new standards link closely with the performance indicators and benchmarks used by HMIE when inspecting state-supported services. For instance, the six criteria for Standard 5 (viz. *Each child or young person can experience and choose from a balanced range of activities*) are already embedded in what is expected as best practice in a nursery environment in all three sectors. In particular, the first criterion for Standard 5 links closely to the requirements of HMIE:

> Children and young people can experience and choose from programmes and day-to-day activities that are planned, designed, evaluated and put into practice by staff taking account of national and local guidelines. (Scottish Executive, 2002b, p 17)

Figure 6.1: The national early education and daycare standards in Scotland

Category	Standard
Being welcomed and cared for	1. Each child or young person will be welcomed, and will be valued as an individual
	2. The needs of each child or young person are met by the service in a safe environment, in line with all legislation.
	3. Each child or young person will be nurtured by staff who will promote his or her general well-being, health, nutrition and safety.

Confidence in the service	4. Each child or young person will be supported by staff who interact effectively and enthusiastically with him or her.
	5. Each child or young person can experience and choose from a balanced range of activities
	6. Each child or young person receives support from staff who respond to his or her individual needs.
	7. In using the service, children, young people, parents and carers experience an environment of mutual respect, trust and open communication.
	8. You will be treated equally and fairly.
	9. You can be confident that the service contributes to the community and looks for opportunities to be involved in the community.
	10. You can be confident that the service keeps up links and works effectively with partner organisations.
	11. Each child or young person has access to a sufficient and suitable range of resources.
Confidence in the management	12. Each child or young person receives support and care from staff who are competent and confident and who have gone through a careful selection procedure
	13. You can be confident that the service will evaluate what it does and make improvements.
	14. You can be confident that you are using a service that is well managed.

Source: National Care Standards — early education and childcare up to the age of 16, Scottish Executive, 2002b.

Somewhat more controversial is the issue of staffing in early years settings. Standard 4 of the new care standards specifies the qualities expected of staff: *Each child or young person will be supported by staff who interact effectively and enthusiastically with him or her.* The four criteria associated with the Standard have clear educational implications. For example, it is expected that staff will:

> Regularly assess the development and learning of each child and young person; use this assessment information to plan the next steps in the child or young person's development and learning. (Scottish Executive, 2002b, p 16)

Assessing and planning children's learning has long been part of the role, though by no means exclusively, of trained teachers registered with the General Teaching Council for Scotland (GTCS). As nurseries in the public sector are no longer required to employ a qualified teacher, the task of assessing and planning learning will become the province of nursery nurses in all these sectors.

The Educational Institute of Scotland (EIS) has expressed its concern at the threat to quality in nursery schools and classes if teachers are no longer mandatory. At the EIS conference in June 2002, delegates on the platform claimed that nurseries in the public sector were in danger of being 'reduced to a baby-sitting service'. Clearly, the stance adopted by the EIS has not changed since 1989 (see Chapter 1). Unfortunately, the evidence for this claim to date is somewhat equivocal. On the one hand evidence from the community nursery research in Strathclyde (see Chapter 1) and the evaluation of quality standards in SINA nurseries (Wilkinson & Stephen, 1998) clearly shows that nurseries run by experienced and competent staff with a nursery nurse qualification and supported by continuing professional development can maintain a nursery environment on a par with good nurseries in the public sector.

However, HMIE reports (see Chapter 5) revealed that nurseries in the public sector which, until now, have all been managed by a qualified teacher, were given higher gradings in all seven of the benchmark criteria than nurseries in the private sector where a teacher is not normally employed. Thus the work of the Commission in regulating the activities of nurseries will be crucial to this ongoing debate. An illustration of the tensions ahead arose in a private nursery in Dundee in 2002. The nursery installed a system for allowing parents to keep an internal eye on their children if they had any concerns. In response, the Commission claimed that major legal and human rights issues had to be considered as potential surveillance of staff was involved. It took months for the Commission to give the go-ahead whilst remaining opposed to the use of web cameras in nurseries. (Scotsman, 11 October 2002). The incident raised questions of trust between parents and professionals, as it is inordinately difficult to regulate in such a domain as this.

6.3 A challenge to the co-ordination of services?

Given the emergence of a powerful new body — the Care Commission — in early childhood education and care in Scotland, with its emphasis on care, it is pertinent to anticipate what role this body might play in the promotion of better co-ordinated services for children and their families. Although 'co-ordination' is not specifically identified as a primary purpose of the new Care Commission, the need for co-ordination of services is identified in Standard 10 (viz. *You can be confident that the service keeps up links and works effectively with partner organisations*). Co-ordination, however, is the dominant theme of the Scottish Executive's policy in its report *For Scotland's Children* (Scottish Executive, 2001a).

This lengthy but much-needed report is an important step forward in the provision of all children's services in Scotland, not just those in the early years. Many different professional groups can be involved with families with young children, particularly those in health and education services. The report recognises that the collaboration between such services in the past has been poor:

> For most children, the health service is replaced by education as the main non-family guide. It is clear that the NHS and education services do not always perceive themselves as having this key role with the child, since there is no handover of responsibility for the co-ordination of services from the NHS to education as a child enters formal education services. For some this loss of continuity is critical. (Scottish Executive, 2001a, p 14)

But for many families health and education are not the only professional agencies involved. Social Work, Police, Children's Panel, Psychological Services and occasionally Child Psychiatrists can also be necessary.

Such a cacophony of professionals can sometimes generate a quagmire of delays and difficulties even for the most disadvantaged of children deemed to have the greatest need, with no agency accepting ultimate responsibility. Parents can feel confused and devoid of empowerment.

The report *For Scotland's Children* contained an Action Plan with six points for action and 12 recommendations. In virtually all the recommendations the Scottish Executive is charged with spearheading the way forward for improving the co-ordination and collaboration between services. In particular, the report supported the proposal for a Children's Commissioner for Scotland. The Executive has agreed that the Commissioner's work will focus on promoting and safe-guarding children's rights, communicating with children and investigating areas of concern such as child protection.

As far as early childhood education and care are concerned, the report highlights the opportunities for better co-ordination under the Sure Start programme, a targeted inter-professional resource for families with very young children.

6.4 Sure Start Scotland

Sure Start is a Government sponsored scheme to support vulnerable families mainly with children under 3 years of age. It is part of a broader strategy *to promote social inclusion through a positive start in young children's lives*. Sure Start Scotland has four broad objectives. They are:

• to improve children's social and emotional development
• to improve children's health
• to improve children's ability to learn
• to strengthen families and communities.

The scheme was launched in 1998, first of all with a letter to the Chief Executive in all local authorities followed by the publication of Guidance to local authorities on Ministers' aims and objectives regarding the expansion of support to families with very young children (i.e. under 3 years old) (Scottish Executive, 1999b). Initially £42M was allocated to the scheme. On the experience of the first year of operation of the scheme revised Guidelines were issued in 2000 (Scottish Executive, 2000c).

Sure Start has a clear educational perspective, as articulated in the Guidance:

> The focus is the promotion of personal growth and development of the very youngest children (0–3) before they have the opportunity of pre-school education. But the child develops within the family, with the well being and broad skills of parents fundamental to a child's progress. This initiative is therefore aimed at providing community based, family focused resources, including high quality childcare and direct support to parents, which through a variety of mechanisms will strengthen parents' ability to maximise their children's potential. (Scottish Executive, 2000c, p 3)

The emphasis in the Sure Start initiative is on the *integration* of services:

> Local authorities and health bodies and relevant organisations in the voluntary and private sectors are asked to work together to meet the objectives of Sure Start Scotland. (Scottish Executive, 2000c, p 1)

However, it needs to be recognised that the effective integration of different services — public, private and voluntary — is not unproblematic (see, for example, Wilkinson, Kelly and Stephen, 1993). Even in the public sector, different agencies have different cultures, different conditions of service and different perspectives. It is important therefore that skills in negotiation and communication are deployed to the full if integration of services is to be realised. Considerable experience is now beginning to accumulate in best practice for collaborative work for vulnerable young children. The work of Abbott and Moylett (1997a) in Manchester offers pointers to such best practice. Strenuous efforts are also being made to train different professional agencies to focus their expertise and work together (see Abbott and Moylett, 1997b).

However, promoting learning and development for very young children (that is, under 3's) is a relatively new field for local authorities. Hitherto the responsibility for supporting young children's well-being was the province of Health Visitors. They have a legitimate role in advising and helping parents both in an ante-natal context and in a post-natal context. If local authorities are expanding their own role under the Sure Start initiative it is vital that NHS Health Boards and the local authorities (both Social Work and Education) are effectively co-ordinated. One such example is in Ayrshire.

The Fit Ayrshire Babies Project (FAB) is a joint initiative between East, North and South Ayrshire Councils and Ayrshire and Arran NHS Board. It aims to promote the benefits and importance of exercise and physical play for very young children and their carers. A wide range of professionals work with a group of very young vulnerable children and their parents who have been identified as the focus of their collaborative initiative.

In its first year (that is, 2001–2002) the project was based in the eight local authority nurseries which offered places to children under the age of three years. In subsequent years it was extended to the other pre-school providers in the private and voluntary sectors, including childminders. The project is jointly funded by the Health Board and the Sure Start programme.

An evaluation of the initial stages of the Sure Start scheme, commissioned by the Scottish Executive, was undertaken at the Centre for Research on Families and Relationships in the University of Edinburgh. In their report Cunningham-Burley et al. (2002) provide evidence of uptake of Sure Start activities ranging from nursery, playgroup and crèche facilities to outreach and mobile services.

In terms of the number of children supported by Sure Start Scotland, the figures rose from 9,155 in 1999/2000 to 15,420 in 2000–2001 (Cunningham-Burley et al., 2002). It is therefore clear that a significant number of vulnerable young children are being supported by this scheme.

The report also shows that in many local authorities joint inter-agency services have been established. However, the evaluators concluded that in the initial stages:

> The opportunities, then, for collaborative working, the sharing of expertise and the development of integrated services across sectors have not yet been fully developed. (Cunningham-Burley et al., 2002, p 24)

Inevitably, expanding the role of the state into the care and education of very young children raises critical issues about the impact of such expansion. In the 1980's a major controversy erupted when Belsky's analysis of research produced the conclusions that *early and extensive non-maternal care carried risks in terms of increasing the probability of insecure infant-parent attachment relationships and promoting aggression and non-compliance during the toddler, pre-school and early primary school years.*

This finding, not unexpectedly, challenges the metamorphosis that has taken place in what Belsky refers to as *the childrearing landscape.* Women now routinely return to work in the first year after having a baby. Such a trend is regarded as sound feminist practice whereby the existence of equal opportunities between the genders to be economically active should not be impaired to any major degree by the reproductive process. Belsky, therefore, is not exactly regarded as the 'beacon of progress' by contemporary feminists.

The findings of Belsky's work, however, cannot be ignored, despite the inevitable frustrations. In terms of its implications for policy and practice in the education and care of young children, further consideration now needs to be given to the expansion of parental leave, preferably paid, along the lines of practice in some Scandinavian countries. As Belsky puts it:

> One of the interesting questions that only history will answer is whether the cost of such leave will prove less than the consequences of its absence. (Belsky, 2001, p 856)

Unfortunately, we cannot wait for the answer to Belsky's question. In the expansion of new territory for the state in the education and care of very young children, vulnerable or otherwise, it is essential that different professional agencies not only collaborate in new ways but work with the parents to support them in their parental role.

CHAPTER 7

TAKING STOCK

7.1 Introduction

Since 1997 Scotland has witnessed groundbreaking policies in the provision of education and care for children under the age of 5. The Childcare Strategy, the Curriculum Framework, Sure Start and the Care Commission are the bedrock of these policies. They were introduced by the Labour Government at the end of the 1990s and subsequently endorsed by the Scottish Executive, a coalition between Labour and Liberal Democrats. They are a watershed in redefining the role of the state in relation to families with young children, a redefinition that endorses regulation and control. This trend is not merely a characteristic of modern Scotland; the entire UK is affected, as is the United States:

> It is indisputable that the child-rearing landscape has changed greatly in the English-speaking world over the past several decades. This is particularly so in the United States, but true in the United Kingdom as well. (Belsky, 2001, p 845)

In these circumstances it is essential to reflect on whether the leap forward in state control acts in children's best interests. It is not in dispute that children need to be protected from the harm that can be inflicted by a minority of adults and other children. Nor is it disputed that the caring professions should learn to collaborate more effectively. But children also need to be brought up in a society that cherishes freedom, flexibility, creativity and responsibility. Unfortunately, there is a real danger that the tiny number of horrific and subsequently sensationalised cases of abuse of children in Britain will provide legitimisation for enhanced regulation by the state and over-protection by parents. It would be catastrophic for the future of Scotland if the well-intentioned regulatory frameworks for the education and care of young children introduced since 1997 inadvertently provided a platform for a new paternalism where the authoritarian forces of restriction inadvertently generated isolation, frustration and fear. But how can such a situation be avoided? What strategies do we have available? One such strategy is to re-visit our conceptions of childhood and to re-assert how diverse childhoods might flourish in contemporary society. The starting point for this strategy is to be found in the work of Rousseau, a French philosopher writing in the eighteenth century.

7.2 The legacy of Rousseau

It is generally accepted in post-enlightenment Scotland that Jean Jacques Rousseau's *Emile*, published in 1762, was a beacon for parents and professionals alike, not in the sense of a quick-fix 'Dr Spock-type' manual in child-rearing but as a catalyst for the nourishment of thoughtful and sensitive relationships between adults and children.

> *Emile* is an account of the development of a fictious eponymous pupil who is in the care of a tutor (effectively Rousseau himself). The guiding principle throughout is that what is to be learned should be determined by an understanding of the child's nature at each stage of his development. (Darling, 1994, p 6)

All those who work with young children, including parents, should be aware of Rousseau's work. It is commonly regarded as the foundation of progressive theories in education, in particular the child-centred movement. Central to this movement is the critical role of 'experience'. According to Rousseau nature has implanted in the child certain instincts for activity and engagement with the world that promote the child's development. *Emile* gives us clues as to how the child's experiences can and should be managed by the adult in the pursuit of the child's happiness. The child *should not be subjected to threats, punishments and other vexations*.

The publication of *Emile* in 1762, according to Darling, *had an electrifying effect*. It was so threatening to much of the established order at that time that copies of the book were burned in the streets of Paris!

Nevertheless, the progressivist movement took hold and the ideas can be traced through to contemporary policies and practices in early childhood education in Scotland via Pestalozzi, Dewey, Froebel and Piaget. Running throughout these theorists is the emphasis on nature. Each child is regarded as having certain 'natural' instincts that must be allowed expression and given recognition and support. As Darling puts it:

> Froebel admired much of what he saw: the nature walks, the games and songs, the conception of education as development, the attempt to base education on the nature of the child. (Darling, 1994, p 20)

The emphasis on nature in progressivist theory led to the growth of developmental psychology in the US and Europe during the twentieth century. Developmental psychologists have been striving to identify universal characteristics of childhood. According to James, Jenks & Prout (1998): *The single most influential figure in the construction of the model of the naturally developing child is Jean Piaget*.

There is little doubt that Piaget's epistemological theory based on natural and universal biological processes has been very influential with nursery nurses and early years teachers. At the core of the theory is the assertion that all children, irrespective of culture, colour or creed, pass through a series of clearly defined developmental and universal age-related stages from birth to adolescence. The role of education was interpreted as facilitating the development of children from one stage to another — from the sensory motor stage to the pre-operational, to the operational and finally to the stage of formal operations associated with the mature adolescent and adult. Embedded in Piaget's 'age and stage' theory is the notion of 'readiness'. According to the theory, if a child has not reached a given developmental stage the child is not ready to learn concepts at the next stage. This notion of readiness still has a strong influence today and is often used in the debate about the optimal age at which children should start primary school.

However, over the past twenty years or so there has been a growing dissatisfaction with Piaget's theory (see, for example, Donaldson, 1978), not least because it has been demonstrated that children possess crucial competences long before Piaget would have us believe. Educationalists have increasingly turned to the work of the Russian psychologist, L.S. Vygotsky, whose theory is based on the notion that children's learning and cognitive development are socially mediated, that is, subject to the influence of social phenomena in the child's external world as opposed to natural, internal biological processes. This does not mean to say that biological pre-programming is not important. Clearly, internal processes are at work in human growth, both intellectually and physically. However, according to Vygotsky, children's intellectual growth and the emergence of 'mind' reflect *their cultural experiences and their opportunities for access to the more mature who already practise specific areas of knowledge*. (Wood, 1988, p 25). Vygotsky's work is now often cited as a source of ideas for early childhood educators and forms the basis of the new socio-cultural psychology as outlined by Anning and Edwards (1999) (see Chapter 4) as a means of supporting children's intellectual journey.

One of the central concepts in Vygotsky's theory is the idea of the 'zone of proximal development'. This zone refers to the gap between what a child is able to achieve alone and what the child can achieve with the support from a more informed other. It is at this time that the mediating role of the educator as 'other' is crucial as the 'messages' transmitted from the educator serve to embed in the child's mind a confidence in dealing with new knowledge and understanding. How the educator therefore delivers these messages becomes crucial to the child's future, whether the message be located in behaviour (for example, role modelling) or whether they be verbal messages. Such language transforms the way in which children learn, think and understand (Wood, 1988). It therefore becomes essential that the educator is fully aware of the role of language — both formal and informal — in shaping children's learning in every sense — not just learning about the world but learning about self and others, which is a central feature of Golman's concept of 'emotional intelligence' (Golman, 1996). Unfortunately Vygotsky's theory is sometimes used to justify more instructional modes of learning, which if taken to extreme lengths can put children in situations that are too demanding, with consequences for their well-being.

Acknowledging that children's learning and development is more subject to cultural influence than had been previously thought has profound implications for education. Parents, teachers and nursery nurses have a renewed responsibility to be more sophisticated in their interactions with children where greater awareness and time for reflection are paramount. Whilst the psychological theories of Piaget, and more recently, Vygotsky may help early years professionals to manage children's learning experiences in the context of the overt curriculum, children are subject to cultural influences often less visible and less formal, yet potentially more powerful in children's construction of themselves, a process that helps to generate diverse childhoods.

Now that the vast majority of 3- and 4-year olds in Scotland attend an early years setting, these settings have a significantly enhanced role in society. It is not inappropriate to ask, therefore, what images of childhood are being transmitted by families and early years settings to our young children being brought up in contemporary Scotland. Deeply embedded in our culture are powerful images of children that play on our emotions. They range from what James et al. (1998) refer to as the *evil child*, the *innocent child*, the *immanent child* and the *unconscious child*. The concept of the evil child has its roots in the religious dogma of the 16th century. In those days children were seen as being born evil and, as a consequence, had to be trained to be good:

> Children...enter the world as wilful material energy...demonic, harbourers of potentially dark forces which risk being mobilised if, by dereliction or inattention, the adult world allows them to veer away from the 'straight and narrow' path that civilisation has bequeathed them. (James et al., 1998, p 10)

According to this view, even in modern times, if children are left unsupervised for any length of time 'badness' could ensue. Perhaps this is why adults are ready to label children as being 'naughty' at the first signs of anti-social behaviour in order to prevent the emergence of something more sinister.

Running through the discourse on this view of children is the proposition that there are dangerous places for children to be — both private, for example, the home of a dysfunctional family, and public, such as busy shopping areas — which could precipitate the emergence of evil forces inherent in the child. Unless accompanied by an adult children are therefore to be kept away from such places less they engage in evil acts. Perhaps the most disturbing of such behaviour in recent times was the murder of James Bulger:

> Since the murder of two-year-old James Bulger in 1993, the child-hood faces of Robert Thompson and Jon Venables have often featured in the tabloids alongside taglines such as 'freaks of nature' and 'products of the devil'. (Barker, 2002, p 569)

We shall never know what motivated Thompson and Venables to behave in such sadistic and lethal acts. But were they evil? Were they the 'monsters in our midst'?

Barker draws to our attention that our society is *particularly shocked and intrigued by the concept of evil children*, yet the number of cases of recorded child murderers remains very low. According to Sereny (1995), only 31 cases of child murder have been reported in the last 250 years. On the other hand, perhaps Thompson and Venables were not freaks but for some unknown reason engaged in sadistic acts that went too far, acts that are more commonplace amongst children than most of us would be prepared to acknowledge. Given that child murderers tend to be male, maybe we should ask: Does the construction of masculinity in our culture encourage disproportionate levels of male violence? Clearly this is a matter for early childhood educators to be more aware of in their day-to-day dealings with young children.

Contrary to this view of children is the image of the *innocent child*. In this discourse children are seen as naturally good, with an intrinsic pre-disposition to be joyful, happy and pleasing, *with an illuminating halo*. Such innocence, it is often thought, has to be protected at all costs from potential corruption and violence in the external world. But does our pre-occupation with preserving such a romantic notion of childhood impede children's natural and spontaneous curiosity? According to Barker:

> We need to question our unrealistic notion of childhood as a time of pure innocence, since when this is violated, demonisation and lack of understanding tend to follow. (Barker, 2002, p 571)

Nevertheless, the image of the innocent child still has a powerful influence over how adults treat children — particularly if the adults are the parents. As such, adults are less ready to acknowledge their child's guilt where wrong-doing has occurred.

James et al. also refer to the concept of the immanent child. Here children are regarded as being born as 'tabula rasa', that is, with nothing other than an immanent potential for growth: *children do not possess inbuilt or a priori categories of understanding or a general facility to reason* (James et al., 1998, p 16). Instead children must be taught such facilities. Having its origins in the work of the philosopher John Locke, writing in the seventeenth century, such a view of children has spurned an approach to education that is based on instruction. Young children are seen as empty vessels to be filled with knowledge and reasoning. However, it is Rousseau rather than Locke who is acclaimed as the source of child-centred education visible in present day early years settings in Scotland. It might be no accident that, being a Frenchman, Rousseau has had more influence on Scottish education than Locke, though Hartley (1993) disputes this claim. The special relationship between Scotland and France, often referred to as the 'Auld Alliance', has ensured greater cultural exchange of ideas between the two countries than between Scotland and England (MacDougall, 2001).

The fourth model of childhood prevalent in our culture is the notion of the *unconscious child*, which has its origins in the work of Sigmund Freud.

> Within the model, childhood is once again dispossessed of intentionality and agency. Instead these are absorbed into a vocabulary of drives and instincts, with sexuality becoming the major dimension in the development of self.... (James et al., 1999, p 21)

This image of childhood sees children as a source of unconscious energy which, if thwarted to any major extent, results in deviant and potentially abnormal behaviour. In many respects it mirrors the view of Rousseau in his unbounded enthusiasm for children's unquestionable and often insatiable curiosity to be channelled positively, though, as James et al. point out, it has done little to *broaden our understanding of children* beyond notions of the 'id', the 'ego' and the 'super-ego'. Nevertheless, such images of children force us to balance our psychological knowledge of children with the growing body of sociological theory. As Hartley concludes in his book on bureaucracy in nursery schools:

> Unless the education of those involved in early education moves beyond its present preoccupation with psychology, it will limit their capacity to engage fully in the policy debates to come. (Hartley, 1993, p 148)

7.3 Childhood in a sociological context

The fundamental distinction between a psychological approach and a sociological approach to the understanding of human conduct is between an individualistic perspective and a group perspective. The former searches for explanations and understandings within individuals, recognising that individual behaviour is a complex interplay of nature and nurture, whilst the latter explores the social world of institutions and structures as a source of explanation. Until recently the dominant theme in the 'social world of institutions and structures' has been the process of socialisation: *Through socialisation individuals learn their society's priorities.* (Scimecca, 1980, p 5).

Socialisation is regarded as the process through which children conform to social norms, roles and expectations, a view which rejects a singular commitment to processes rooted in nature:

> The socially developing model is not therefore attached to what the child naturally is, so much as to what society naturally demands of the child. (James et al., 1999, p 23)

The process of socialisation is seen by many sociologists as key to our understanding of different childhoods. At the core of such a process is the family, specifically the role models transmitted, often inadvertently, by the adults and siblings in the family. For example, if children display anti-social behaviour, the starting point for an explanation of such behaviour is in the behaviour of adults and other family members. But the most powerful group processes at work in shaping children's minds are those concerned with divisions in the wider society — age, gender, social class, disability and ethnicity. Such differences are often associated with prejudice and inequality. As such, they are hurdles to human progress by acting as barriers to greater awareness, understanding and tolerance.

On the matter of prejudice in age difference, or 'ageism', as it is sometimes referred to, given that children, by definition, are younger than adults and thereby thought to be less competent, less experienced, less knowledgeable and less wise, there is an assumption that adults necessarily know what is best at all times. Adults often unconsciously exert their power and authority over children with little thought for the consequences. Unfortunately, the physical and psychological abuse of children inside the family is still all too prevalent and authoritarianism has a bad habit of being perpetuated across the generations. Fortunately, there are early indications that the tide is beginning to turn in that more attention is now being paid to hearing 'children's voices'. The establishment of a Children's Council in Glasgow is to be welcomed so long as it is given a role that is not tokenistic. All those who work with children should spend more time 'listening' to their voices and respond appropriately.

Gender is another issue of keen relevance for early years educators as it is a central defining feature of people throughout the world. Very often from birth very young children are stereotyped into male and female roles. 'Blue for boys and pink for girls' is but the tip of the iceberg in the messages about male/female roles transmitted often unconsciously to our children.

> Some children are locked into traditional conceptions of gender while others are able to move partially towards a more liberated view of gender, where their social environment includes women who are active agents in the world, where there are men who have undertaken a significant proportion of the nurturing female roles, and where they have been free to practise non-traditional behaviours in an environ-

ment where this is taken to be the normal thing to do. (Davies, 1987, p 56)

Davies argues that it is essential for early years educators to liberate children from traditional stereotype roles and to help children become aware of their non-maleness if they are boys and their non-femaleness if they are girls. There are increasing signs that society is finding ways of liberating girls but has failed so far to find ways of similarly treating boys.

If progress is now visible in tackling genderism, at least for girls, little progress has been made in addressing the social class issues in our society. This matter, however, is perhaps less straightforward in the context of early childhood education and care. Whilst children may be very aware at an early age of their gender identity there is no extensive evidence that they are also aware of differences in life chances. Social inclusion may be the goal of the Scottish Executive's policies but translating the goal into day-to-day practices in an early years setting is not unproblematic, though respect for diversity and the promotion of equity and fairness must be central. Despite the fact that there is a strong association between socio-economic status and educational achievement, any assumption that a child's background inevitably determines the child's intellectual capabilities must however be challenged.

The issue of racism is a somewhat different matter. Siraj-Blatchford clearly articulates the issues for children and for those who educate and care for them in a pluralistic society such as modern Britain:

> The most common form of racism young black children experience is through racist name-calling or through negative references by white children (or adults) to their colour, language or culture. (Siraj-Blatchford, 1994, p 9)

But racism is not merely restricted to overt behaviour of individuals. Increasingly, we are becoming aware of institutional racism, which is more subtle and persuasive. Such a form of racism is embedded in the policies and everyday practices in our institutions and public life. In response, early years educators have been prompted to devise racial equality policies that go beyond multicultural education. In the culturally responsive early years setting, the curriculum should:

- foster children's self-esteem
- acknowledge the cultural and linguistic backgrounds of all children
- actively maintain and develop the children's first or home languages
- promote the learning of English as an additional language
- value bilingualism as an asset
- support families in their efforts to maintain their languages and culture
- challenge bias and prejudice

- promote a sense of fairness
- promote principles of inclusion and equity

(Siraj-Blatchford, 2001, p 106)

The fifth source of tension in our society and of considerable relevance to early years professionals is the issue of disability, which includes children with special educational needs. The key issues are illuminated in an earlier book in this series by Riddell (2002). Under the influence of current policies on inclusion, progress is being made to engage children with disabilities in mainstream early years settings. But much remains to be done.

All children, irrespective of their race, creed, colour, disability or status, have a right to be treated with dignity and respect. Such a 'right' is enshrined in Article 2(1) of the United Nations Convention on the Rights of the Child which states:

1. The States Parties to the present Convention shall respect and ensure the rights set forth in the Convention to each child within their jurisdiction without discrimination of any kind, irrespective of the child's or his or her parents' or legal guardian's race, colour, sex, language, religion, political or other opinion, national, ethnic or social origin, property, disability, birth or other status.
2. States Parties shall take all appropriate measures to ensure that the child is protected against all forms of discrimination or punishment on the basis of the status, activities, expressed opinions, or beliefs of the child's parents, legal guardians or family members.

More recently, attention has been drawn to other considerations in the sociology of childhood which helps to enhance understanding of how society treats children. This emerging body of sociological theory is often referred to as the new sociology of childhood. James et al. (1998) refer to such concepts as the *socially constructed child* and the *tribal child*. In the former, sociologists de-construct the common assumptions about childhood as being a distinct and absolute form of the human lifespan. Instead, they point to childhood as a product of its time and material conditions by placing it *squarely in the realm of the culturally located and thus humanly constituted.*

On the other hand the idea of the tribal child is regarded as a recognition of the separateness of childhood with codes, language and rituals somewhat different from those of adults. Children often have their own way of doing things which other children understand. Such tribalism can act as a source of mutual support in adverse situations and often has expression in children's play, particularly when it is unsupervised by adults.

Both concepts are of considerable significance to early years educators. Not only do they require nursery teachers and nursery nurses to be more aware of the assumptions inherent in their own attitudes and behaviour towards children but also to be aware of the tribal culture at work so that they can engage with it more meaningfully.

7.4 The New Agenda Revised

The attention given by the UK Labour Government and the Scottish Executive to early childhood education since 1997 is to be wholeheartedly welcomed. Robust and penetrating policies have been backed up with the necessary resources. The policies implemented since 1997 which are outlined in this book, however, have carried different messages to those involved in the education and care of children in the early years, both professionals and parents. In the late 1990's the policy initiative was predominantly 'educational'. The creation of national curriculum guidelines in the form of the *Curriculum Framework for Children 3–5* emphasised that children's learning was at the centre of the early years experience. In addition, some local authorities — particularly those established after the disaggregation of Strathclyde Region — took the step of integrating pre-school services into one administrative department, that is, the Education Department or its equivalent.

Not everyone welcomed this trend. Concerns were voiced not only about the needs of vulnerable children not being sufficiently well addressed in a traditional educational environment such as a nursery school, but also about the needs of parents wishing to be economically active. In order to establish a balance between the promotion of learning for all children (the 'universality' principle) and the channelling of appropriate support to children 'at risk' (the 'targeting' or 'vulnerability' principle) the new Care Commission was given the remit of regulating early years settings.

It is difficult to reconcile the principle of universality with the principle of targeting. In the early years of the new millennium, the pendulum has swung in the direction of protecting vulnerable children. Whilst this is understandable given recent events, the trend is not unproblematic. The ultimate test of the effectiveness of any educational experience has to be located in the process of modernisation. Such is the challenge of the new agenda in early childhood education in Scotland.

But this is not all. The way forward requires a new level of professionalism that enshrines the need to address in a sensitive but purposeful manner the social divisions in the wider society outlined earlier in this chapter. Promoting awareness, understanding and tolerance is the very heart of the educative process and it begins in the early years of life.

All those who work with young children require to be attuned to the new challenges and responsibilities they now face. The first years of life are critically important, a fact recognised long ago by the Jesuits in the famous phrase: *Give me the child till he is seven and I will give you the man.*

The policies put in place under New Labour since 1997 provide early childhood educators and administrators with a daunting opportunity. No longer is early childhood education a luxury for the few: it is in the vanguard for all.

REFERENCES

Abbott, L. and Moylett, H. (eds) (1997a) *Working with the Under 3s: responding to children's needs*, Buckingham: Open University Press.

Abbott, L. and Moylett, H. (eds) (1997b) *Working with the Under 3s: training and professional development*, Buckingham: Open University Press.

Anning, A. and Edwards, A. (1999) *Promoting Children's Learning from Birth to Five*, Buckingham: Open University Press.

Balaguer, I., Mestres, J. and Penn, H. (1992) *Quality in Services for Young Children*, Brussels: Commission of the European Communities.

Ball, C. (1994) *Start right — The Importance of Early Learning*, London: Royal Society of Arts.

Barker, M. (2002) The evil that men, women and children do, *The Psychologist*, 15(11), pp 568–571.

Belsky, J. (2001) Development Risks (Still) Associated with Early Child Care, J. Child Psychol. Psychiat., 42(7), pp 845–859

Berrueta-Clement, J.R., Schweinhart, L.J., Barnett, W.S., Epstein, A.S. and Weikart, D.P. (1984) *Changed Lives — The Effects of the Perry Preschool Program on Youths Through Age 19*, Monograph No. Eight of the High/Scope Educational Research Foundation, Ypsilanti: High/Scope Press

Black, P. and Wiliam, D. (1998) *Inside the Black Box*, London: School of Education, King's College.

Blair, A. (1998) Foreword by the Prime Minister in *Meeting the Childcare Challenge — A Childcare Strategy for Scotland*. Edinburgh: The Scottish Office.

Bowlby, J. (1952) *Maternal Care and Mental Health*, Geneva: World Health Organisation.

Brown, S., Stephen, C. and Low, L. (1998) A Research Analysis of Pre-School Provision in the Market Place, *Scottish Educational Review*, 30(1), pp 4–14.

Carew, J.V. (1980) Experience and Development of Intelligence in Young Children at Home and in Day Care. Monographs of the Society for Research in Child Development, 45 (6–7), Serial No. 187.

Central Statistical Office (1995) *Social Trends*, 25, London: HMSO.

Children Act (1989)

Clarke-Stewart, A. (1991) *Day Care in the USA*, in Moss, P. and Melhuish, E. (eds) Current Issues in Day Care for Young Children,

London: HMSO.

Cohen, B. (1988) *Caring for Children*, London: Family Policy Studies Centre.

Cohen, B. and Fraser, N (1998) *Childcare in a Modern Welfare System*, London: Institute for Public Policy Research

Cunningham-Burley, S., Jameson, L., Morton, S. Adam, R. and McFarlane, V. (2002) *Sure Start Mapping Exercise*, Edinburgh: Centre for Research on Families and Relationships.

Dahlberg, G., Moss, P. and Pence, A. (1999) *Beyond Quality in Early Childhood Education, and Care*. London: Falmer Press

Darling, J. (1994) *Child-Centred Education and its critics*, London: Paul Chapman Publishing Limited.

Davies, B. (1987) The Accomplishment of Genderdness in Pre-School Children, in Pollard, A. (ed), *Children and their Primary Schools — a New Perspective*, London: The Falmer Press.

Department of Education and Science (1990) *Starting with Quality*, Report of the Committee of Enquiry into the Quality of the Education Experience offered to 3- and 4-year olds (The Rumbold Report), London: HMSO.

Dewar, D. (1998) Introduction by the Secretary of State for Scotland, in *Meeting the Childcare Challenge — A Childcare Strategy for Scotland*, Edinburgh: The Scottish Office

Donaldson, M. (1978) *Children's Minds*. London: Fontana.

Dowling, M. (2000) *Young Children's Personal, Social and Emotional Development*. London: Paul Chapman Publishing Limited.

East, North and South Ayrshire Councils (2001) *Fit Ayrshire Babies*, Ayrshire: East, North and South Ayrshire Councils.

Eccleshall, R., Geoghegan, V., Jay, R. and Wilford, R. (1984) *Political Ideologies*, London: Hutchinson.

European Commission Network on Childcare (1996) *Quality Targets in Services for Young Children*, Brussels: Commission on the European Communities

Galbraith, S. (1999) Foreword, in *The Child at the Centre*, Edinburgh: Scottish Executive.

Giddens, A. (1998) *The Third Way*, Cambridge: Polity Press.

Giddens, A. (1999) *10th Economic and Social Research Council Lecture*, London: ESRC.

Giddens, A. (2000) *The Third Way and its Critics*, Cambridge: Polity Press.

Glasgow Herald (2002) Are you sure your child is safe in their hands? Glasgow: *Glasgow Herald*, 04.10.2002.

Golman, D. (1996) *Emotional Intelligence*, London: Bloomsbury Publishing Plc.

Golombok, S. (2002) Why I study lesbian mothers, *The Psychologist*, 15(11), pp. 562–563.

Golombok, S., Perry, E. , Burston, A., Murray, C., Mooney-Somers, J., Stevens, M. and Golding, J. (2002) Children with Lesbian Parents: a Community Study, in *Developmental Psychology* (in press)

Harms, T. and Clifford, R.M. (1980) *Early Childhood Environment Rating Scale*, New York: Teachers College Press.

Harms, T. Clifford, R.M. and Cryer, D. (1998) *Early Childhood Environment Rating Scale* (Revised Edition), New York: Teachers College Press

Hartley, D. (1993) *Understanding the Nursery School*, London: Cassell.

Henwood, M., Rimmer, L and Wicks, M. (1987) *Inside the Family: changing roles of men and women*, London: Family Policy Studies Centre

HM Inspectorate of Education (2002) *Standards and Quality in Scottish Pre-School Education 1997–2001*, Edinburgh: HMIE.

House of Commons *Achievement in Primary Schools*, Vol. 1, Third Report from the Education, Science and Arts Committee, London: House of Commons.

Howes, C. (1992) *Caregiving environments and their consequences for Children: the experience in 4 United States*, in Melhuish, E. and Moss, P. (eds), Day Care for Young Children – International Perspectives. London: Routledge.

James, A., Jenks, C. and Prout, A. (1998) *Theorising Childhood*. Cambridge: Polity Press

Kelly, B. (1995) Children, families and nursery provision, *Early Child Development and Care*, 108, pp 115–136.

MacDougall, N. (2001) *An Antidote to the English — the Auld Alliance, 1295–1560*, East Linton: Tuckwell press

McCartney, K. (1984) Effect of Quality Day Care Environment on Children's Language Development, *Dev.Psychol*, 20(2).

McLanahan, S. and Sandefur, G. (1994) *Growing Up with a Single Parent*, Cambridge, M.A.: Harvard University Press.

Moss, P. (1990) *Childcare in the European Communities 1985–1990*, Brussels: Commission on the European Communities

Moss, P. (1995) Foreword, *Early Childhood Development and Care*, 108, pp 1–4.

Moss, P. and Penn, H. (1996) *Transforming Nursery Education*, London: Paul Chapman Publishing Ltd.

Moss, P. and Melhuish, E. (eds) (1991) *Current Issues in Day Care for Young Children*, London: HMSO.

Muncie, J., Wetherall, M, Dallos, R. and Cochrane, A. (eds) (1995) *Understanding the Family*, London: SAGE

New, C. and David, T. (1985) *For the Children's Sake*, London: Penguin Books.

Osborn, A.F. (1994) There are long term benefits of Early Education: but is this the right issue? *Education Section Review*, 18(2), pp 57–60.

Pence, A. and Moss, (eds) (1994) *Valuing Quality in Early Childhood Services* London: Paul Chapman Publishing Limited.

Penn, H. (1988) Information paper 22: The Strathclyde Pre-Fives Policy: Development and Debate, *Scottish Educational Review*, 20(2) p 118–120.

Penn, H. (1992) *Under Fives: The View from Strathclyde*, Edinburgh: Scottish Academic Press.

Phillips, D., McCartney, K. and Scarr, S. (1987) Child-Care Quality and Children's Social Development, in *Developmental Psychology*, 23(4), pp 537–543.

Pugh, G. (1988) *Services for Under Fives: Developing a Co-ordinated Approach*, London: National Children's Bureau.

Pugh, G. (ed) (2001) *Contemporary Issues in the Early Years*, London: Paul Chapman Publishing Limited.

Regulation of Care (Scotland) Act (2001)

Renfrewshire Council (2001a) *A Report on Standards and Quality in Pre-Five Nurseries in Renfrewshire – Partner Nurseries*. Paisley: Renfrewshire Council.

Renfrewshire Council (2001b) *A Report on Standards in Pre-Five Nurseries in Renfrewshire – Council Nurseries*, Paisley: Renfrewshire Council.

Riddell, S. (2002) *Special Educational Needs*, Edinburgh: Dunedin Academic Press.

Roll, J. (1992) *Lone Parent Families in the European Community*, London: European Family & Social Policy Unit.

Scimecca, J. (1980)

Scotsman (2002) U-turns as care agency gives green light for nursery webcam link, *Scotsman*, 11.10.2002.

Scott, G. (1989) *Families and Under Fives in Strathclyde*, Glasgow: Glasgow College.

Scottish Education Department (1965) *Primary Education in Scotland* (The Primary Memorandum), Edinburgh: HMSO.

Scottish Education Department (1971) *Before Five*, Edinburgh: HMSO.

Scottish Education Department (1972) *Education in Scotland: A Statement of Policy* (Cmnd 5175), Edinburgh: HMSO.

Scottish Education Department (1987) *Curriculum and Assessment in Scotland: a Policy for the 90's*, Edinburgh: SED.

Scottish Executive (1999) *Guidance on Sure Start: Scotland*, Edinburgh: Scottish Executive.

Scottish Executive (2000a) *The Child at the Centre – Self Evaluation in the Early Years*, Edinburgh: Scottish Executive.

Scottish Executive (2000b) *Regulation of Early Education and Childcare – The Way Ahead*, Edinburgh: Scottish Executive.

Scottish Executive (2000c) *Sure Start Scotland: Guidance (Revised June 2000)*, Edinburgh: Scottish Executive.

Scottish Executive (2001) *For Scotland's Children*, Edinburgh: Scottish Executive.

Scottish Executive (2002a) *Summary Results of the 2002 Pre-school and Daycare Census*, Edinburgh: Scottish Executive.

Scottish Executive (2002b) *National Care Standards — early education and childcare up to the age of 16*, Edinburgh: Scottish Executive.

Scottish Executive (2002c) *Child Protection Statistics for the Year ended 31 March 2002*, Edinburgh: Scottish Executive

Scottish Office Education Department (1994) *Education of Children Under 5 in Scotland*. Edinburgh: SOED.

Scottish Office Education Department (1995) *Using Performance Indicators in Nursery School/Class/Pre-Five Unit Self Evaluation*, Edinburgh: SOED.

Scottish Office Education and Industry Department (1996) *Improving Achievements in Scottish Schools*, Edinburgh: HMSO.

Scottish Office Education and Industry Department (1997a) *A Curriculum Framework for Children in their Pre-School Year*, Edinburgh: Scottish Consultative Council on the Curriculum.

Scottish Office Education And Industry Department (1997b) *Education in Early Childhood: the Pre-School Years*, Edinburgh: Scottish Office Education and Industry Department.

Scottish Pre-School Play Association (1997) *SPPA Standards and Indicators of Good Practice for Sessional Playgroups*, Glasgow: Scottish Pre-School Play Association.

Sereny, G. (1995) *The case of Mary Bell: A portrait of a child who murdered*. London: Pimlico.

Shorrocks, D. (1993) Seven-year-olds assessed, *Concern* (Autumn, 1993).

Siraj-Blatchford, I. (1994) *The Early Years — Laying the Foundations for Racial Equality*, Stoke-on-Trent: Trentham Books Limited.

Siraj-Blatchford, I. (2001) Diversity and Learning in the Early Years, in Pugh, G. (ed) *Contemporary Issues in the Early Years*, Third Edition, London: Paul Chapman Publishing.

Stephen, C. and Wilkinson, J.E. (1995) Assessing the quality of provision in community nurseries, in *Early Child Development and Care*, 108, pp 83–98.

Stephen, C. and Wilkinson, J.E. (1996) *SINA Quality Assurance Scheme*, Glasgow: Department of Education, University of Glasgow.

Stephen, C., Low, L., Brown, S., Bell, D., Cope, P., Morris, B. and Waterhouse, S. (1998) *Pre-school Education Voucher Initiative: National Evaluation of the Pilot Year*, Stirling: Department of Education, University of Stirling.

Stephen, C., Brown, S., Cope, P. and Waterhouse, S. (2001) *All-day Provision for 3- and 4-Year Olds: The experiences of children, parents, providers and practitioners*, Stirling: Department of Education,

University of Stirling.

Strathclyde Regional Council (1985) *Under Fives: A Member/Officer Group Report*, Glasgow: Strathclyde Regional Council

Sylva, K. (1991) Educational Aspects of Day Care in England and Wales, in Moss, P. and Melhuish, E. (eds), *Current Issues in Day Care for Young Children*, London: HMSO.

Sylva, K. et al. (1999) *Characteristics of Pre-school Environments*. Technical Paper 6a, Effective Provision of Pre-school Education (EPPE) Project, London: Institute of Education.

Sylva, K. and Wiltshire, J. (1994) The impact of early learning on children's later development, in *Education Section Review*, 18(2), pp 47–55

The Scottish Office (1998a) *Meeting the Childcare Challenge – a Childcare Strategy for Scotland*. Edinburgh: The Stationery Office Limited.

The Scottish Office (1998b) *New Community Schools Prospectus*, Edinburgh: The Scottish Office.

The Scottish Office (1999a) *A Curriculum Framework for Children 3–5*, Dundee: Scottish Consultative Council on the Curriculum.

The Scottish Office (1999b) *Regulation of Early Education and Childcare – A Consultation Paper*, Edinburgh: The Scottish Office

The Scottish Office (1999c) *Targeting Excellence – Modernising Scotland's Schools*, Edinburgh: The Scottish Office.

Tennant, R. (1995) *Child and family poverty in Scotland: the facts*, London: Save the Children, and Glasgow: Glasgow Caledonian University.

Tisdall, C. and Donaghy, E. (1995) *Scotland's Families Today*, Edinburgh: Children in Scotland.

Tymms, P. (1996) *Baseline Assessment and Value-Added*, London: Schools' Curriculum and Assessment Authority.

Watt, J. (1990) *Early Education: The Current Debate*, Edinburgh: Scottish Academic Press.

White, P. (1999) Political Education in the Early Years: the place of civic Virtues, in

Wilkinson, H. (1998) The family way: navigating a third way in family policy, in Hargreaves, I. and Christie (eds), *Tomorrow's Politics: The Third Way and Beyond*, London: Demos.

Wilkinson, J.E. (ed) (1995) Community Nurseries: Integrated Provision for Pre-Fives, *Early Child Development and Care*, 108, pp 1–160.

Wilkinson, J.E, Kelly, B. and Stephen, C. (1993) *Flagships: an evaluation of community nurseries in and Strathclyde Region 1989–1992*, Glasgow: Department of Education, University of Glasgow.

Wilkinson, J.E. and Napuk, A. (1997) *Baseline Assessments – a Review of Literature*, Glasgow: Department of Education, University of Glasgow.

Wilkinson, J.E. and Stephen, C. (1998) Collaboration in Pre-School Provision in Scotland: Promoting Quality in the Private Sector. *Early Years*, 19(1), pp 29–38.

Wilkinson, J.E., Watt, J., Napuk, A. and Normand, B. (1999) Tracking Children's Progress: Record Keeping in the Pre-School Year, in Wilson, V. and Ogden-Smith (eds) *Pre-School Educational Research: Linking Policy with Practice*. Edinburgh: Scottish Executive Education Department.

Wilkinson, J.E., Johnson, S., Watt, J., Napuk, A. and Normand, B. (2001a) Baseline Assessment in Scotland: an Evaluation of Pilot Procedures, in *Scottish Educational Review*, 33(1), pp 33–47.

Wilkinson, J.E., Johnson, S., Watt, J., Napuk, A. and Normand, B. (2001b) Baseline Assessment in Scotland: an analysis of pilot data, in *Assessment and Evaluation*, 8(2), pp 171–192.

Wilkinson, J.E., Baron, S. and Schad, D. (2002) *An Evaluation of the Integrated Services Unit at Lochend New Community High School*, Glasgow: Department of Educational Studies, University of Glasgow.

Wilson, B. (1997) Foreword, in *Education in Early Childhood: The Pre-School Years — A Consultation Paper*. Edinburgh: The Scottish Office.

Wood, D. (1988) *How Children Think and Learn*, Oxford: Basil Blackwell.

Useful website addresses
Scottish Executive Education Department: *http://www.scotland.gov.uk*
The National Care Commission: *http://www.carecommission.com*
Learning & Teaching Scotland: *http://www.ltscotland.com*
HMIE: *http://www.scotland.gov.uk/HMIE*